Ambroise Matignon, Constance Bellingham

Duties of Christian Parents

Ambroise Matignon, Constance Bellingham

Duties of Christian Parents

ISBN/EAN: 9783337300333

Printed in Europe, USA, Canada, Australia, Japan

Cover: Foto ©Lupo / pixelio.de

More available books at **www.hansebooks.com**

DUTIES OF CHRISTIAN PARENTS.

DUTIES OF CHRISTIAN PARENTS.

BY
R. PÈRE MATIGNON.

Translated from the French,
BY
LADY CONSTANCE BELLINGHAM.

With a Preface by
THE RIGHT REV. MONSIGNOR CAPEL, D.D.

LONDON:
R. WASHBOURNE, 18 PATERNOSTER ROW.
1879.

TRANSLATOR'S NOTE.

THE Conferences now given to the English public were delivered in Paris some ten years ago, and owe their origin to the desire of certain heads of families to receive special advice and instruction upon the solemn duties of their state regarding the management of their households and the education of their children.

The Jesuit Fathers of the Rue de Sèvres undertook to give them these instructions, and the celebrated Père Felix of that Order, more than once preacher of the great Lenten Conferences of Notre Dame, presided at the first meetings; but being called away from Paris in the autumn of 1867, he was succeeded by the Père Matignon, the author of the present Conferences.

It is necessary to state that the Translator has,

with the permission of the author, omitted a few pages of the Third Section of the Seventh Conference, the subject of which, treating as it does of the division of inheritance according to the law of France, would scarcely be applicable in England, where the same law rests upon quite a different basis.

The present volume of Twelve Conferences is complete in itself, but in 1877 and 1878 the series was continued. The latter conferences compose two volumes which may at some future time be translated into English.

C. B.

January, 1879.

PREFACE.

THE present age is one of progress in the material order, of discovery in physical science, of useful inventions, of diffusion of knowledge, yet perhaps there never was a time when it was more necessary to revert to those first principles which lie at the foundation alike of individual perfection and of the moral well-being of society.

Among such fundamental principles, there is none more important in its nature or more extended in its application than the principle of authority. All lawful authority is from God; that which is not directly or indirectly derived from Him, is usurped and tyrannical. It is a trust, a sacred stewardship, of which He will require an account. This is admirably expressed in the important Encyclical just published by our Holy Father, Pope Leo XIII., against Nihilism and

Socialism.* "It is plain," says the Sovereign Pontiff, "that the Church does wisely in impressing upon the many subject to authority the Apostolic precept: *There is no power but from God; and those that are, are ordained of God. Therefore he that resisteth the power, resisteth the ordinance of God. And they that resist purchase to themselves damnation.* And again he admonishes those *subject by necessity* to be so *not only for wrath but also for conscience' sake,* and to render *to all men their dues; tribute where tribute is due, custom to whom custom, fear to whom fear, honour to whom honour.* For He who created and governs all things, has in His wise Providence ordained that all should occupy their proper places, the lower beneath the middle, the middle below the highest. As, therefore, in the heavenly kingdom itself He has decreed that there should be distinct orders of angels, some subject to others; and as in the Church He has instituted various orders, and diversity of offices, not all being Apostles, or Doctors, or Pastors; so also has He appointed that there should be in civil society many orders, dis-

* From the *Tablet.*

tinguished by their rank, privileges, and power; so that the State, like the Church, should be one body, comprising many members, some more noble than others, but all mutually necessary, and all concerned for the common good."

Pre-eminent amongst all authorities derived from God stands that of the head of the family—the husband and father, to whose keeping is committed the material and in some measure the spiritual welfare of wife and children. This authority is the very key-stone of home, and of that family life on which the strength and greatness of a nation mainly depend. We cannot do better than cite again from the same Encyclical: "Even that domestic relation which is the foundation of all society and government necessarily feels and experiences the salutary influence of the Church in the orderly regulation and preservation of civil society. For you know, Venerable Brethren, that the true principle of this society is to be found in the first instance in the indissoluble union of husband and wife according to the necessity of natural law, and is perfected in the mutual relations and obligations of parents and children, masters and servants. You know also that this principle is almost destroyed by the doctrines of Socialism; for, when that stability which is imparted to it by religious marriage is lost, it necessarily follows that the authority of fathers over their children and the duty of children to their parents, are greatly relaxed. But the Church, on the contrary, teaches that *marriage, honourable in all*, which God in the very commencement of the world ordained and decreed to be indissoluble for the propagation and preservation of the human race, was made still more binding and holy by Christ, who gave it the dignity of a Sacrament, and willed that it should be a type of His own union with His Church. Wherefore, as the Apostle teaches, as Christ is the head of the Church, so the man is the head of the woman; and as the Church is subject to Christ, who embraces her with a chaste and perpetual love, so also should wives be subject to their husbands, and be loved by them with faithful and constant affection. So likewise does the Church enjoin the moderate exercise of paternal and domestic authority, that without exceeding due bounds, it may control children and

servants in the discharge of their duty. . . . . .
For, according to Catholic teaching, the authority of the heavenly Father and Master is deputed to earthly fathers and masters; which, therefore, not only derives its origin and force from Him, but acquires another nature and character. Hence the Apostle exhorts children to *obey their parents in the Lord, and honour their father and mother, which is the first commandment with promise,* and he admonishes parents: *And you, fathers, provoke not your children to anger, but bring them up in the discipline and correction of the Lord.* Again the Apostle lays down to servants and masters the divine precept, exhorting the former to be *obedient to their lords according to the flesh as to Christ— with a good will serving, as to the Lord:* and the latter, to *forbear threatenings, knowing that the Lord of all is in heaven, and there is no respect of persons with God.* And if these things were diligently performed in accordance with the Divine will by all to whom they are commanded, the family would present as it were an image of the heavenly home, and the blessings flowing therefrom would not be confined within the walls of private

dwellings, but would spread with the greatest abundance throughout the nations."

In olden days parental authority was venerated in our land: nowhere were the bonds of the family drawn closer, or the influences of home life more deeply felt. Although much was swept away by the spirit of anarchy which the so-called Reformation introduced, yet the deeply-rooted Catholic idea of home remained, interwoven, as it were, in the very being of our race, and was the admiration of foreign nations.

It cannot but be a matter of grave and anxious concern to those who look thoughtfully at the present state of society amongst us, to see that family life is losing its sacred character, that the respect for conjugal and parental authority has diminished, and that home is no longer the place to which men and women instinctively turn for their earthly rest and happiness. We see evidences of this change in the legalising of divorce; in the substitution of a merely civil contract, made before a Registrar, for the religious and sacred bond of matrimony; in the assumption of the parental office by the State in the matter of education; in the separation of secular and religious instruction; in the avoiding or postponement of marriage, consequent on the habits of luxury which have come to be considered as a necessity of our day; in the readiness on the part of fathers and mothers to transfer to others the nurture and education of their children from their earliest infancy; and in the precarious relations existing between masters and servants.

Of the evil physical effects of the relaxation and partial subversion of parental authority, a painful and striking testimony is given in the tenth chapter of Doctor Tuke's valuable work on "Insanity in Ancient and Modern Life."

France for a century has been passing through her bitter trial; the Revolution, in the name of Liberty, Equality, and Fraternity, swept over the land, crushing religion and wrecking the idea of paternal authority; her military conscription has attenuated, if not severed, the sacred bond of family life. A change has come, and now France seeks her regeneration. This can only be accomplished by a due recognition of the divinely appointed rights and duties of that authority which is the foundation of all true liberty. Her devoted Christian Teachers diligently and earnestly labour to lay down, as the only true and lasting basis of National Life, the solid principles on which the family is divinely established.

One of the many wise and experienced priests who have dealt with this important subject is Père Matignon, a member of the great Society of Jesus, which has long been conspicuous by its learning, its accumulated experience, and its skill in the guidance of consciences. His valuable instructions, which were originally given at the monthly meetings of French fathers of families, in the Jesuit Church, Rue de Sèvres, Paris, are now placed within the reach of English readers generally, with the earnest desire that they may tend to the conservation of the old and beautiful Catholic home life of England.

If among our labouring classes the parental and conjugal authority, described in these instructions, with its correlative of due obedience and respect were housed in material homes marked by cleanliness, order, and brightness, we should have the strongest and most durable barrier against that widespread intemperance which is the great curse of our people.

T. J. CAPEL.

Feast of the Epiphany, 1879.
CATHOLIC PUBLIC SCHOOL, KENSINGTON.

CONTENTS.

FIRST CONFERENCE.
RIGHTS OF GOD OVER THE FAMILY . . . 1

SECOND CONFERENCE.
UNITY OF IDEAS IN THE FAMILY . . . 24

THIRD CONFERENCE.
UNITY OF IDEAS IN THE FAMILY.— THE OBSTACLES TO THIS UNITY 47

FOURTH CONFERENCE.
UNITY OF IDEAS IN THE FAMILY (CONTINUED).— THE MEANS TO ATTAIN IT 66

FIFTH CONFERENCE.
UNITY OF AFFECTION IN THE FAMILY.— THE CENTRE, POSITION, AND QUALITIES THAT IT SHOULD POSSESS   85

SIXTH CONFERENCE.
UNITY OF AFFECTION IN THE FAMILY (CONTINUED).—THE BOND WHICH UNITES THE MEMBERS TO THE CENTRE 107

SEVENTH CONFERENCE.

UNITY OF AFFECTION IN THE FAMILY (CONTINUED).
—NECESSITY OF RELIGION TO PROTECT THEM . 131

EIGHTH CONFERENCE.

UNITY OF FAMILY LIFE.—OBSTACLES—THE RELATIONS 146

NINTH CONFERENCE.

UNITY OF FAMILY LIFE (CONTINUED). — OBSTACLES—
THE TWO FAMILIES 165

TENTH CONFERENCE.

UNITY OF FAMILY LIFE (CONTINUED). — OBSTACLES—
DIVERSITY OF CHARACTERS . . . 185

ELEVENTH CONFERENCE.

UNITY OF FAMILY LIFE (CONTINUED). — OBSTACLES—
DIVERSITY OF TASTES 209

TWELFTH CONFERENCE.

UNITY OF FAMILY LIFE (CONTINUED). — OBSTACLES—
PLEASURE 236

DUTIES OF CHRISTIAN PARENTS.

FIRST CONFERENCE.

RIGHTS OF GOD OVER THE FAMILY.

The idea of forming a Society destined exclusively for the study of the great duties of parental relationship, is one evidently inspired by God.

It was felt how useful and beneficial it would be for heads of families to assemble under His eye, and join their hopes, fears, and troubles in common, and how it would assist men in strengthening one another by the force of example and the consideration of the one object proposed to all.

For this reason a series of familiar conferences was suggested which would have no other aim than to explain the sacred duties involved in the title of parent.

With the aid of the light of Faith, we will then begin a practical review of our duties, and endeavour to ascertain the best method of fulfilling them.

In order that these studies should have a solid basis, we must from the outset call to mind the principle upon which everything rests, a truth as positively certain as it is nowadays disregarded and forgotten, and yet one which, though it should be engraved in indelible characters on the frontispiece of every dwelling, is now rarely to be met with, even amongst nominal Christians. This truth, even if it should recur from time to time theoretically in their minds, in most instances remains unfruitful as far as regards the government of life. The first question will be, to whom does the family belong?

Is man, as head of the family, to be considered as its legitimate and real proprietor, because it is in its physical and perhaps also in its moral character but the extension and continuation of himself?

Or is he the representative of rights superior to his own?

Does he administer, not in his own name, but in that of another, a possession which is not his, and which he cannot, without crying injustice, take or claim as belonging to him? This is the question that comes before us at the very beginning of our considerations, and to this question Christianity makes a clear and peremptory answer, destroying every exaggerated pretension, and defying every subterfuge. We need not fear that it will deprive the human Fatherhood of its greatness, which, on the contrary, is its safest bulwark against ruin; for paternal dignity can compromise itself quite as much in striving to usurp what does not belong to it, as in disregarding its own true prerogatives and necessary privileges. Let us leave it in the position where Nature has placed it, and consider its dignified office and its providential action.

Parental authority is seated upon a throne—a borrowed one, it is true, but one none the less elevated or respected.

The power thus exercised is neither independent nor absolute, but subordinate and relative. In order to understand it, we must go back to the source from whence it comes, and of which it is only a partial and incomplete representative. Let us then consider, first, what are the rights of God over the family, and, secondly, draw general conclusions as to the position resulting therefrom for those who have the honour to bear the name of father. The subject is too vast to admit of our doing more, in this conference, than forming, in one comprehensive view, a general idea. We will consider the different component parts at our leisure in the series of conferences that are to follow.

I.

The human family has at its head a man who is called its chief, and yet that family cannot be regarded as his own possession or personal property. Nothing is more clear than this, if we allow words to retain their natural meaning; for every intelligent creature belongs to its Creator, and forms a part of the prerogative of God; and that prerogative is essential, exclusive, and for ever inalienable.

Such is the fundamental principle laid down by reason and faith. But this principle, however incontestable, is not and cannot be sufficient for us. We are not studying isolated beings, but the family in its multiplied nature and collective existence: the family with the organisation that distinguishes it and the hierarchy inseparable from it; the family which is a homogeneous society, a living and harmonious body, a being with a life and individuality distinct from any other. Such did the family issue forth from the hands of God; such must it return to Him, without disregard of those rights, the basis of which is consecrated in its own constitution.

This law appears to be forgotten, and indeed almost universally ignored. Where shall we look for the house that either respects it, that accepts it seriously, or admits the logical consequences that flow from it? And yet, if the family does lose sight of this law, it is because it is deficient in memory, and because it does not know how to go back to the mystery of its origin.

Let us consider a moment the first page of the Sacred Scriptures. After each preliminary creation, we see the Divine Maker of the world congratulate Himself upon the work, which He hails with a transport of admiration. "*Vidit Deus quod esse bonum :*" "God saw that it was good." Words of deep meaning, which science corroborates every day, the more it penetrates into that abyss of marvels which it will never succeed in completely fathoming.

Man is the masterpiece of creation, and yet after he had been created, God did not repeat those words. It seems, on the contrary, He regarded the work as imperfect; He declared that it was not good to leave man in his present state. "*Non est bonum hominem esse solum :*" "It is not good for man to be alone." It was only after the formation of woman from the very flesh of her companion—that is to say, when the family began to appear in its necessary unity and dualism—that God declared Himself satisfied and, contemplating as a whole the beings He had called into existence, proclaimed their incomparable beauty. "*Vidit Deus cuncta que fecerat, et erant valde bona :*" "God saw what He had made, and it was very good." Here we have the culminating point of the Divine work, that which completes it, and gives it its final stroke and lustre.

Everything that had been made before was to terminate in man; and man himself was not complete save in the domestic society which held in itself the germ of every other, an association blessed and privileged, to which Heaven forthwith undertook to give a constitution. This constitution, promulgated as it was from the first day of the existence of the world, was already then so perfect, that afterwards, when the fallen family had to be re-established, regenerated, and all that had been shipwrecked in the deluge of pagan corruption to be restored, Jesus Christ could do nothing better than recall it to its first type, and to the fundamental law promulgated at the birth of innocent humanity. It is not my intention at present to insist on this great fact. I wish one thing to be borne in mind, viz., that nothing in the family is left to arbitrary decision; everything concerning it has been regulated by Nature, that is to say, by the Divine Creator of the universe Himself. Divine right may have been abolished elsewhere: here it is to be found in all its strength and beauty; not one of these magnificent duties are of man's invention; not one place in the domestic hearth is otherwise than is pointed out by the finger of God; not one hierarchical degree that was not established at the beginning by Him from whom all things depend, and to whom they owe a tribute of homage. With regard to civil society, a number of details have been left undetermined. Nations make to themselves their institutions, or if they receive them already made, it is by the irresistible power of events, or by the predominance of the human will, which nothing is capable of counterbalancing. Such, however, is not the case with the family. The legislation of this primeval society has been fixed since the beginning of the world. Its code is co-equal with itself. There is no doubt that its meaning can be falsified, and that ignorance and pagan degradation can change and distort many of its maxims, but these maxims remain written not only in the Sacred Scriptures, but also in that other book which man deciphers for himself, when the social atmosphere he dwells in has not completely blinded him. I mean that universal book of instinctive feelings, and spontaneous affections, to be found amongst every people and in every place. There are moralists nowadays who would fain establish a radical distinction between the family of olden times and that of the present day; who declare that the French Revolution of 1793 has severed in two not merely social existence, but also domestic life. We have, therefore, two theories. On the one hand the "*ancien régime*," with its principle of authority seated in the home as well as on the throne; on the other the new and plausible one, with its principle of liberty both in political institutions and in private relationships.

In following this course of conferences, we shall have occasion more than once to discuss these modern assertions; for the present it will suffice to say that we must beware of these two opposite views, and of these exclusive divisions. It is immaterial whether changes have taken place or not in civil governments. Nature knows of none such. The child is born with the same rights and the same wants, the father remains invested with the same attributes and the same duties. Doubtless there may be some accidental modifications from the fact that the spirit of the times must be taken into consideration, and, after all, it is the future generation which has to be formed, but the family remains to-day what it was yesterday. It will not be able to fulfil the mission it has received either by means of unlimited authority or unbounded liberty, but must accomplish its work by evenly administering and wisely moderating the one and the other, whilst keeping its eye bent, not on itself or its own gratifications, but upon society, to whom it supplies members, and upon God, whose glory it must seek to advance. In short, the father is an administrator, not a proprietor. The Creator, who might have dispensed with his co-operation, has thought well to make him His confederate in the greatest and most important work of all, the most critical and the most difficult, viz., the production and formation of man; that is, in other words, the coming into existence and the shaping of a soul, and its preparation for the great destinies that await it. Such is the common enterprise undertaken both by God and the family. Both the one and the other are interested in this work, if I may venture to use the expression, in almost equal proportions; both also exercise in it a necessary influence, imprinting upon the living production that is about to issue from their hands their own image and resemblance; for, without denying the part which falls to our individual liberty, it can yet be affirmed that each one of us is the fruit of the combined action of God and the family. A natural contrast is thus established between these co-operators. In addition to that General Providence which directs all things, we cannot but recognise between God and domestic society a more intimate alliance, and a more continuous and more attentive direction. It is this that constitutes the dignity of the married state, and here we also see the admirable harmony of the teaching of our Faith. Why, otherwise, does God intervene, at the moment the family is formed with a special sacrament?

Why, when it is increased, does He come in again

not only through His creative act, which remains invisible, but, further, by a regenerating act, having an outward and material symbol. Christian marriage and baptism mark two solemn epochs; they are in fact epochs when the Almighty, in a special manner, takes possession of the family, and imprints His seal on each of its additions, evident proofs that He looks upon it as His sacred and inalienable property.

We know that no transaction can be concluded when the party principally concerned is absent. Human law, whilst it has the charge of looking after the rights of all men, has a special disposition to ward off this peril; it requires the presence of the injured party, or at least a regular or solemn representative. Need we be surprised that Christian law should bring the same exigencies into another order of things.

Where is the party principally concerned in the contract which we find at the basis of the family? Is it not God Himself? Society established between man and woman cannot be complete unless He is joined to it; it cannot be either holy or legitimate if He is not Himself its bond and the very cause of its existence. The family, however, in modern times is, unfortunately, too often under the exclusive inspiration of earthly and worldly cares, Almighty God is either not consulted, or not called to witness its commencement. Ambition, money, passion, or pleasure alone preside over a decision replete with irreparable consequences; some alliances are formed which religion only blesses with a trembling and faint heart; others exist which it has not even sanctioned. Hence comes an irremediable falling off in the family; for in excluding God from itself, it excludes with Him its morality, its strength, and its only guarantee of happiness.

We cannot but see in this fact a deep and radical evil in the domestic society of our days. Civil society is in part responsible by obstinately disregarding, as it does, the essentially religious character of marriage, and bringing it down from the heights upon which Nature and Christianity have placed it to the level of a purely secular contract. Let the state register accomplished facts; let it concern itself about patrimonies, doweries, and inheritances, but let it be clearly understood that the state does not and cannot effect marriages, and that it has received from no one the power of binding or loosing the individual.

Furthermore, neither our denials nor our usurpations can destroy the rights of God. The human family, from the mere fact of repudiating God, is none the less His property, or possesses any the less the sacred duty of working for Him, and of conforming to His sovereign intentions. And let us take special notice that God requires of the family not merely individual homage, rendered personally by each of its members, but that He requires of it as a society a collective worship, a common profession of faith, a form of prayer in which, gathered in one voice, are to be heard the voices and hearts of all; a submission to Divine law as shown forth by the presence of all in the holy place on certain days, and a due conformity between its faith and practice.

Let no one reply, The greater number of our modern Societies abstain from connecting themselves with religion, and prefer to leave to each of their members freedom of worship; why should not the case be the same with the family? It is not necessary for me to discuss here the principles of our constitution. "Roma locuta est;" "causa finita est." We know that it is not in political transactions that we must look for an ideal order, or for absolute right; but whatever be our judgment upon the existing state of things, there can be no comparison made between the duty of our governments and that of the father of the family. Domestic society, as we have just stated, depends in no wise upon the will of man; its existence and its constitution are a fact both natural and divine, and its mission is traced by the Creator, whose action it represents, and whose work it continues and completes. To try and effect a divorce between parties so essentially connected, is both a crying injustice and even a sin against Nature itself. These rights must not only be affirmed, but enforced, and then, willingly or unwillingly, we are compelled to recognise them.

Should, for instance, the Almighty take away, in whole or in part, the fortune He had bestowed, the family must not murmur or complain of Providence, as if Heaven were committing an act of injustice; but must rather exclaim, as did that most afflicted of all parents: " The Lord gave, and the Lord hath taken away; blessed be the name of the Lord :"*
"*Dominus dedit, Dominus abstulit; sit nomen Domini benedictum.*" It may be as with the great sufferer in Holy Writ: God will not only ask back of some of you whom I am addressing, wealth, but perchance a son or several sons—treasures a thousand times more precious, though only lent to their parents on this earth; and yet you may have concentrated on them your affections, placed in them your hopes, and looked upon them as a beloved property over which you alone had any right. But now you see arise before you a superior right, that of death, which is truly but the faithful messenger and interpreter of the Divine Will. The Author of life shows Himself armed with the supreme power belonging to Him as His due, and then forgetful and blinded tender-

* Job i. 21.

ness has to learn, amidst a flood of inconsolable tears, who alone is the true Proprietor of the family, and who alone the sole Judge and Disposer of all the human race.

At other times the Almighty, without using His omnipotence so rigorously, appears under the aspect of a Pleader, and contents Himself with indicating, in a tender and almost timid voice, the designs of love He has formed for a life scarcely beginning to expand. He will ask of a father and mother a kind of previous authorisation to pour forth His blessings; He will ask them to let one of their sons or daughters be called to honours and joys which the world would try in vain to bestow upon them. The table may indeed be already adorned, and the banquet prepared, and the happy guest hastening to seat himself by the side of his spouse. And yet a refusal is often given. The call from on high is looked upon by the father as a threat, and the invitation of Heaven as an intolerable demand: Why should the Almighty dare to take away from father and mother a possession belonging exclusively to them? How can God be allowed to make good His claims upon that son whom the parents had already predestined for a prosperous earthly career? The family remonstrates, and makes opposition; it would consider itself unjustly deprived of its own, were it not to give to the world what it holds most dear. The right of

God is thus disregarded, denied, and perhaps even blasphemed at the very moment in which it asserted itself by a tender and powerful attraction, and displayed before the eyes of youth the prospective of those joys which come of sacrifice, and of those privileged virtues which thrive in the death of earthly affections. The parent may perhaps turn away, as if by force, those looks that were directed towards Heaven; he may even clip the wings of those thoughts, and restrain the impetus of those prayers and aspirations; but it will be a perilous attempt, a dangerous and terrible undertaking, for it will often happen that a heart that has been prevented from giving itself to God, will become filled with unwholesome and guilty affections, and whereas it would have striven to reach sanctity, will now no longer understand even ordinary virtue. I could enumerate many circumstances where the family shelters itself behind its own selfishness, and loses sight of the source from which it obtains everything, and to which it ought to refer back all that had been committed to its charge. All this points to the fact that an energetic and devoted protection is necessary to the rights of God, which are so often forgotten and disregarded. They must have a defender to represent them, to plead for them, and to cause them to triumph. And this defender whom Nature puts forth is not the priest (he indeed is placed too far, his action is only to be felt in the depths of conscience, and too often can exercise there but slight influence), but the father of the family.

II.

The father of the family must be considered the born defender of the rights of God, because all power here on earth brings with it a responsibility. The father is the head of a household, only on condition that he maintains amongst those placed under him the laws of order, which are in fact the laws of God. Man is entrusted on the day in which he becomes husband and father with a sublime mission; he acquires these titles because he represents a Type above him, a more exalted Type of Fatherhood. "*Ex quo omnis paternitas in cœlo et in terrâ nominatur:*" "From Whom every fatherhood in heaven and earth is derived."*

The character with which he is vested is a priesthood, and to this priesthood is given the charge of souls. His wife and children, beloved beings to whom he is attached less by the ties of the flesh than by those of the heart, constitute the blessed flock which are given to him to direct and superintend. Such is the world of which he is the

* Ephesians iii. 15.

centre and the life; and just as in the great world which surrounds us there is a hidden and invisible Providence whose incessant action governs all things, so also in that more restricted but no less beautiful world that is called family is there a Providence always to be felt even when it is veiled, and always on the watch, even when it appears to wish to escape notice: a love imitating in the government it exercises the solicitude of the supreme and universal love, and like it uniting gentleness and strength, mingling in equal proportions the energy which leads to the goal, and the tenderness which facilitates the journey, a graceful and amiable task in which will be found, but in a less proportion, the principal features of that first fatherhood, from which all the subsequent ones are derived. The head of the family has to render an account not merely of himself, but also of those placed under him. One law of nature binds him to beings whom one cannot but regard as a continuation of his existence, and another places them under his moral direction. By virtue of the position he occupies, he has an order of interests far above those of earth entrusted to him; to defend the rights of God must be his first thought, and these rights are often blended with those of human beings. As I have already stated, both of these rights are involved in the greater portion of those questions, which the father is principally called upon to determine. First comes the question of the formation which begins with life, and one which is oftentimes decisive of the whole future. Then what sort of teaching should be given? what system of education should be followed out? what stamp impressed upon Nature? what disposition given to character? in a word, what preparations should be made against the terrible eventualities of existence? Then follows the time when childhood is transformed into youth; what path should be pursued? what society be sought for? what studies encouraged, what amusements permitted? According as these formidable problems present themselves before the family (full of difficulties for the present, and of grave consequences for the future), God must be listened to, and consulted. Will the sacred interests implicated in all these things find a serious defence, and a solemn guarantee, in the attitude taken by the parents? I fear too many are engrossed with every other subject but this; and yet the question here is not only that of the salvation of their children, but also of their morality, their happiness, and their peace, it may even be that of their material prosperity and perhaps of their life.

I cannot at present speak at any length upon any of these truths: I am only taking a general view of a whole, and endeavouring to embrace in one glance the immense extent of the paternal mission. Man is called upon to defend and protect the rights of God not only as regards his children, but also as regards that which is nearest and dearest to him.

The soul of his wife has been confided to him, and all that are seated at his table, live under his roof, and are placed under his authority, resemble the members of a body of which he is the head and the visible providence. The father is the promoter of the fortune, honour, and material well-being of the family; he warmly espouses their cause, he watches the development of growing faculties, encourages efforts and applauds success, and has the power (though often nowadays but a feeble one), to repress what might compromise the earthly destiny of the child or young man. The one thing necessary is too often made light of, and sacrificed to conventionalities, caprice, love of money, ambition, and perchance sensuality; and yet to this one thing all else should yield, since none other presents the same gravity or the same importance. It is impossible for any length of time to protect and watch over interests but those which are sympathetic.

It is impossible to have complete devotion without love, or to find courage to defend a cause as one's own, and to serve it even at the sacrifice of one's self, without becoming identified with it.

In this lies the strength of the father in the administration of the affairs of his house; what labour or trouble will he refuse to undergo in order to increase the inheritance he is preparing for his children? what expenses will appear heavy to him where their health is concerned? what undertaking will he consider too difficult in order to further their interests and their career in life? The reason is that their fortune, their health, and their social standing are to him questions of paramount importance; he can appreciate and embrace these interests, and he thinks he can never do enough to give them full and entire satisfaction. It would be the same with religious interests if they held in his heart the same place as the advantage of this world.

Until, then, you re-establish in your appreciations and affections this essential and invariable order, no matter what proofs of disinterested devotion you have shown in your families, you have not done more than half your duty, or rather it is a proof that you only understand the restricted and narrow side of a father's position, and that you have accomplished only the least and most unimportant part of your exalted office. In order to a complete exercise of the duties of paternity, you must rise to the higher standard, and conform to the Divine Type, of which it has been justly said there could be no equal. "*Nemo tam Pater quam Deus:*" "No one is such a Father as the Almighty." If you aspire at all to this sacred dignity, you must do so on the exact Divine pattern, diminishing none of its prerogatives.

Whoever leaves aside its best part, not only falls himself, but drags everything down with him in his fall; the family descends the steps which the father has refused to mount, and from the very fact of his not possessing the place of honour, which he ought by rights to occupy, everything will probably be relegated to a lower standard. An authority without a solid foundation, and affections without basis, are all that can be installed in the domestic hearth, when the proper functions of the father are thus in abeyance, and in their wake will often come insubordination, anarchy, disorder, and revolt; the authority of the parents will be cast aside, respect will be trampled under foot, and love repaid by ingratitude; the most sacred ties of Nature will be relaxed by indifference, or severed by aversion and antipathy.

If the results are disastrous, and the parent has to deplore the turn of events, let him ask himself did he not begin in the first instance himself to undermine the edifice which it was his duty to erect?

His authority had not the sure basis of a superior power, it did not take its stand upon the inherent right which comes from on high; it was like the house mentioned in the Gospel that was built upon sandy ground, and when the storm came it was reduced to a great ruin, because the foundation being insecure, it could not resist the violence of the shock.

The only means of escaping such dangers is to restore to God His place in the family, should He have been excluded from it, or to yield to Him, if already there, a wider and more secure sphere of influence. Such, in fact, is the first and imperative duty. You who seek to understand the full extent of the responsibility of a Christian father of a family, recognise that it is called to sustain and protect what is greatest upon earth.

For this purpose you have established these meetings, in order to study together, in a more special manner than is done elsewhere, the obligations that are attached to an office so great and so important. Let us therefore beg of God that His light may shine more and more in our actions and on the responsibilities in this brotherly exchange of impressions and feelings, which will be carried on in His sight.

After each conference, may each parent become prouder of his dignity, more convinced as to his duty, more disposed to fulfil it at the cost of every sacrifice; in a word, may he come away from it more completely and truly alive to the important duties he has to perform.

This is the object of our work, on which we implore the Divine blessing.

SECOND CONFERENCE.

UNITY OF IDEAS IN THE FAMILY.

We have seen that the human family is a creation of God, the last in order, and the most magnificent of all His works, and the one which completes the entire scheme of creation as a harmonious whole, in such a way that there is nothing above or below it except what is an indispensable corollary or a merciful development.

Such a production must have its mark, and it is easy to see the hand of God in it, for it is He who imprints upon every marvel that He has produced, the seal of unity.

It is this special characteristic that makes them beautiful, and through it they reflect the image and likeness of their Maker. The more this unity asserts itself, the more powerfully does it sum up in its composition the multiplicity and variety of its elements, the higher does it mount up in the social scale, and the nearer does it approach to absolute perfection.

Nowadays natural science proves more and more this great law in its classification of things; æsthetic sense reveals it to the followers of art; and Saint Augustine long since defined it in the axiom—" *Omnis pulchritudinis forma unita est:*" " The reason of all beauty, and the form which expresses it, is unity."

Now if we except the individual man, the attribute of Divinity is nowhere so clearly visible as in the family. First of all, we find in it material unity. I mean unity of the blood and flesh, for the flesh remains one, though belonging to two persons. " *Duo in carne una:*" " Two in one flesh." The original dualism further resolves itself into one fruitful source which multiplies life. Though at the beginning there are two separate roots, they become one and the same tree, and this tree does not lose its identity when it expends its sap in powerful ramifications, and is crowned with many branches and much fruit.

We have as yet but an exterior unity, a unity in its humblest aspect; but still this unity lays upon the family the most sacred of all duties, and the rending of it would be equivalent to its division and destruction. But I wish to treat of another unity, and one of a higher degree, which must occupy our attention in a greater measure, because on it everything depends, and in it everything is completed; viz., moral unity, the key-stone of the family, the axis upon which everything is based, and round which everything revolves. Where this exists nothing need be feared, and if it ceases to exist, everything is lost. The firmer, stronger, and more complete it is, the more does the family approach its ideal, and the more does it realise the admirable type upon which it was constructed.

This moral unity which we are about to discuss is one that must be examined in all its details with great care, if we wish to trace its origin to the primitive forces which engender it. These forces group themselves in three orders, viz., ideas, affections, and habits of life. Let us consider the first of these at present.

I.

In every society composed of intelligent beings, the only ground for mutual understanding is the harmony established by unity of ideas.

It does not follow from this that, from the moment they come together, minds must be cast in the same mould, and not preserve in any one point the liberty of their divergencies of opinion. The alliances amongst us are far from exhibiting in the same degree, a similar train of thought, and each one has its own special characteristics.

In this way the great human society leaves a

large field for varied schools of thought, opinions and systems, and requires nought else than agreement upon the general interests of humanity, and in each country upon those concerning its own welfare. To restrict the circle still more, where it is only a question of forming a commercial, scientific, or literary association, its members must agree upon the object of the undertaking and the means of success; but nothing need hinder them from having various opinions in other matters. Friendship also is an association, and the amount of thoughts, appreciations, and ways of looking at things that people have in common, generally determines the height to which it will attain. But in the family circle alone harmony becomes absolutely essential. Observe that I use the word harmony, and not unison, for just as in a concert we do not expect or require every instrument to have the same tone, or every note to have the same sound; but on the contrary, a diversity of tones and their apparent dissemblance, which is considered as the height of perfection in a well-modulated score of music; so must it be in the family. It is the numerous parts of the orchestra worked out one by one by a clever composer which charm by the attractions of variety and banish the possibility of monotony. We know that an audience would complain if it heard in the midst of this variety any discord, and that it would groan and hiss if one instrument were to play false, or if one voice were to be heard out of tune. This would be because confusion is never beautiful, but always shocks the instincts of our nature, and is still more objectionable when it shows itself in places where it is least expected.

A little while ago, the discordant sounds in the streets produced no feeling of irritation, but here where we have met together for quiet discussion, they jar on our sensibilities and excite our indignation or annoyance.

So it is in the moral order of things. Certain antagonisms of ideas which would be of no importance amongst strangers, would become serious amongst those living under the same roof, because the peace of the domestic sanctuary would probably thereby be impaired.

Yet nowadays this is an ordinary occurrence. We often find in the family people with opinions widely differing even upon the vital question of religion. I am not now speaking of its practice; some cannot find enough courage in their hearts to be consistent, but yet retain the faith and agree in principle with the belief that surrounds them. But in many cases this belief is entirely wanting. Both the extreme of unbelief and ardent lively faith, both true piety and an open hostility against Christianity, are represented at the same table. Extremes meet. The Catholic creed, and the materialistic profession of faith, perpetually come into contact, and the most irreconcilable ideas are constrained to live side by side.

Is this a happy or a right state of things for the family, or would it not be more logical to assert as certain modern writers have done, that a complete absence of religion is desirable, in order that the family should find unity in indifference or atheism. Unity in atheism! Such a thing can never be, since atheism is a mere denial of all centre, of all fixed point, of all rallying round a principle, and of all order in thought. Unity in irreligion! If such a thing can exist, it will be but deceptive and fatal. Even its advocates tremble to find it in their own homes. They dread to indoctrinate their wives with it, for fear of bringing upon themselves sleepless nights; still less do they teach it to their children, for fear of causing confusion in the household, anarchy instead of authority, and disorder instead of virtue. Even the conflict of ideas and estrangement of individuals on the religious question, must be considered as better than this.

And yet what a series of difficulties will be the consequences of this latter. The family cannot go on in life without a number of practical questions being raised around it, which it is forthwith called upon to solve. And amongst these questions there are few into which religion does not, to some extent, enter, and few to which the Christian conscience can remain a stranger. Whether it is a question of education, or direction, or the choice of friends, or of what pleasures should be allowed, the answer will often differ according as to whether one looks at things from a spiritual or worldly point of view.

What agreement or unity can possibly be expected from a husband and wife who, having a point to decide, the one declares himself incapable of abandoning the first, and the other of abandoning the second?

It may be perhaps brought forward that people can live under a system of mutual forbearance; but would to God that this forbearance were just and true! Would to God that it did not require of the weaker party concessions which conscience repudiates, and which the interests of the family, if well understood, ought unhesitatingly to reject. No one knows what sorrow is stored up in the heart of a mother, obliged to give up her children to an anti-Christian education from which she has but too much reason to expect nought but misery, obliged to give them pleasures prematurely dangerous and corrupting, and liable in one minute to wither the flower she has tended with so much care and nurtured with so much love and solicitude. Placed between duties which are contradictory, she will be perpetually giving way in the interests of peace. A peace of this sort is only on the surface, and though externally everything may be tranquil, there is sure to be some hidden trouble and agitation, and often terrible storms in store for the future.

I am now merely sketching out the principal basis upon which unity of ideas should be established. Everything else is accessory to it! I do not deny that the peace of political and other social spheres may be momentarily disturbed through conflicts of opinion. But the difficulty in this case never goes far; interior tranquillity can never be much compromised. However, it must be admitted, the closer minds are drawn together, even on this purely human ground, the easier will be this union, and the more will the hearts themselves be led to gravitate towards each other, according to the law of invincible attraction.

The father of the family, though respecting legitimate liberty, cannot lose sight of this superior interest: his most ardent wish, or at least his ideal and dream, would be that the inmates of his house should verify the words of the Apostle, that they should have but one thought and one tongue.

II.

Amongst the means which are made use of to accomplish this peace in the family, there are two completely at variance, both equally false and productive only of an outward appearance of unity. It is necessary to point out these two contrary excesses, into which those who have charge of the moral guidance of the family, too often fall. The first is a spirit of dictation exercised in the order of ideas.

Most assuredly it is not my intention here, either to set at nought or to lessen the halo which surrounds the authority of the parent. For even apart from the undisputed power it receives from God, experience, reflection, and a profound knowledge of men and things, assert that it has not only the right, but still more the duty, to undertake the guidance of the intellect, as it already has that of the will and the actions. The father, who is worthy of the name, has solid convictions which he establishes firmly in the young minds he has charge of; it is his task to impress upon them in indelible characters, those truths which at all times constitute the glory of the human race; that belief which will be a bulwark against the temptations of prosperity, and a consolation in the hour of trouble.

It must never be forgotten that the government of minds is both a delicate and a difficult task.

Compulsion alone will be of no avail, save to make truth itself hateful. In order to rectify ideas, persuasion will be necessary; persuasion which not only brightens and encourages, but secures the assent of the intellect, and drives it home by means of those links which rise from the depths of the heart.

But there exist persons who are guided by their own will in place of that of God, failing thereby to perceive that this erroneous condition is like a shadow, and becomes an obstacle in the way of those under them.

These people evidently look on themselves as infallible. They think their ideas alone right, or their views alone reasonable. Whoever hesitates to adopt their sentiments, or refuses to agree with their opinions, is wrong. Every one must think exactly as they do, under pain of incurring their indignation.

Contradiction irritates them, even a simple observation, however modestly and quietly made, suffices to annoy them. A lover of peace will have to accept without examination, and without questioning, every word they utter. Each one of their dictums must be received as the very oracle of truth. This is personal government brought into the family, and established in the very region where it is most unsuitable. For if there be one place more than another where men enjoy as a matter of course a reciprocal independence, it is in truth. The only voice which has power to impose belief, is that inspired by God, that which He has authorised by His promises and which He sustains and consecrates by a special privilege. If the father use his influence to obtain respect for the teaching of those voices, well and good; if himself the first to submit to this doctrinal power, and to teach others to seek there the rule of their thoughts, then will he be wholly in his sphere, and none will be able to charge him with encroaching upon the rights of intellects. He can go even further. He will naturally become the initiator of the young minds who surround him. His wife and children will learn from him what opinion they should hold upon a multitude of things of which they know nothing; and after having fed them with material food, he will willingly place before them that which is more substantial, the fruits of his studies, his meditations, conclusions and experiences. But in all this, the less overbearing he is the greater will be his strength, the more he avoids everything akin to moral constraint, the greater will be the power of his words. Are there not men whose outward demeanour is pleasant and amiable, and whose intercourse with strangers is easy and charming? But no sooner are they in their own houses than a transformation takes place.

Everything that was agreeable and charming gives place to outrageous demands of injustice and intolerance.

Even amongst religious men this spirit is to be found. Such persons are not content that those around them should be Christians unless they act exactly in conformity with their particular standard. Forgetful of the fact that every soul is not constituted alike, they wish to make all the world follow the path they have chosen. Should this path happen to be that of asceticism, the wife and daughters will be obliged to give up certain practices which their more expansive nature deemed necessary for them; should it, on the other hand, be the reverse, they will condemn to it minds whose preference would have been for asceticism.

But there is no need to dwell upon these details. Wherever the spirit of dictation appears, sufferings follow, and are multiplied in its wake. Even though passive obedience may not be wanting, an undercurrent of murmuring and discontent is sure to exist. The silence it demands may be obtained, but it will be constrained and contrary to Nature, covering with an appearance of agreement what is in reality opposed to it; and mouths silenced by fear will reopen as soon as they are free; the longer they are held in subjection, the greater will be the eventual outbreak.

Without taking into consideration the result of a meeting between a despotic character of this sort, and a really independent spirit of determined convictions, which would inevitably result in repeated shocks and, sooner or later, painful collisions; there is a constant source of sadness in the family circle, perhaps even of scandals which appear before the world. What if the dominating spirit, instead of being that of the man, should pass, as it often does, to her whom he has chosen as his partner for life? The drama then presented by the family would be like those plays in which the tragic and the comic are so intermingled, that one never quite knows whether the pathetic or the ridiculous prevails.

In these scenes, the part of the husband who does not dare, in his own house, to express an opinion, is always deplorable. He may be a man lacking neither in energy nor initiative, when by himself; yet at his own home he is silent and depressed. Having to cope with a power stronger than his own, he prefers surrender to constant altercation, and chooses the *rôle* of insignificance rather than perpetual controversy.

We must not omit to notice a still more strange subversion of order, which might be called one of the principal characteristics of our day.

The will, and perhaps also the thoughts, of the

parent are moulded upon the caprice of the child, constituting a tyranny as deplorable as it is short-sighted. Holy Scripture says: "*Væ tibi terra cujus rex puer est;*" "Woe to the people whose king is a child."* Does not this saying apply equally to the family? A stupid and ill-advised affection has overturned its proper condition. Those who should have been on the watch have been asleep, and those who should have held the reins have allowed themselves to be directed. Present deviations the father counts of no consequence. He at first laughs to see in the hands of a youth the sceptre of a reed, which he looks forward to destroying at will, and under which he bends without resistance.

But he must beware; time is advancing, and with years the reed becomes stronger. Should he delay but a little longer, it will change into a rod of iron; and the yoke which he did not throw off in time will eventually prove insupportable.

III.

Some heads of families lay aside altogether the duties and responsibilities of their position. This happens sometimes from dislike to disturbances and quarrelling, from listlessness of character and love of peace. In despair of arriving at a solution, they desert the field of battle and sign a shameful peace.

* Eccles. x. 16.

From that time dates their fall, and the fall is generally without hope of future restoration.

Others give way to weakness of character. Having, in fact, no individuality of their own, they seem to seek nought else but a will to lead them. Would to God they would only find the right one! and that amongst the aspirants who will not fail to come forward, they should not overturn the natural order, and call into existence an irregular authority.

Amongst those causes which bring into the home a multitude of sorrows, we must place in the first rank the jealousies of power and influence; these arise from the partial or entire neglect of duty by the natural heads of the family, and so, whatever may be its motive, such neglect will always bring misery. The father has an important position which he alone can occupy; he has a duty to fulfil which he alone can accomplish, and in which no one can replace him. A family where the head is wanting, and where the salutary impulse flowing from it is no longer felt, can only be compared to a ship without a pilot, or a state without a government.

We may be sure that, in spite of the efforts and devotion of those interested in its destiny, disorder, and anarchy would inevitably ensue. Who like a father can mould the mind of the young, and especially the young man? If no one watches on the threshold, a thousand erroneous ideas, finding the way open, will take up their abode there.

Studies of a suspicious character have first brought them in, rash and senseless statements do not fail to endorse and support them. The choice of reading will be left to chance or dictated by fancy; the elective power of natural attraction is always turned by preference to that which flatters passion. Those writers will be most listened to whose voice is most dangerous, and who falsify principles and instil error in place of truth, who administer subtle and deadly poisons, under the appearance of an innocent potion.

The ideas of the youth are pliable like those new branches of a tree upon which rests the hope of the future; if we unfold them with care, and gently train, without breaking them, we ensure their fruitfulness, and favour their growth. It is a work requiring skill but, above all, love; it becomes, for the most part, impossible not only when paternal discipline is distasteful, but also when it does not assert itself, and when it does not take pains to maintain established order, and to bring back to their normal place those vigorous and untamed branches which, carried away by the force of their sap, threaten to escape from all restraint and discipline.

The family in which the father has abdicated his proper authority soon begins to resemble those virgin forests where vegetation, left to itself, becomes entangled; or to resemble an inextricable labyrinth, through which man can only make his way by fire and sword. The case is the same with individuals: through growing in the same soil—their ideas come into collision, clash, and perhaps stifle one another; it is the struggle for life of which naturalists speak, where the stronger prevails over the weaker, until it dies itself, a victim of its own excesses. Should there be in it any semblance of concord, it will be but fallacious, for, in the absence of all understanding between ideas established in the same home, peace can only exist by means of a diplomatic silence, incompatible with true expansion of character, or in a sort of absolute disinterestedness, too much resembling indifference.

Fathers, what have you done with the priesthood God had confided to you, and which constituted for you a distinct commission? No power could free you of your obligations, for your voice has an accent not to be imitated, and your authority a sovereign power to establish honour and virtue in your children, and to engrave upon their consciences noble and exalted ideas. But, thanks to your guilty abstention, there is no longer in you either tradition or unity.

Like Eli in the Old Testament, you have allowed iniquity to penetrate into the sanctuary; the enemy will come as before, and the ark of the covenant will itself be taken, and upon you will fall the responsibility of those disasters before God, and also before men.

IV.

Since the principle of abstention is as reprehensible as that of arbitrary authority, we must look for another method of preserving intact that concord and unity of mind which should exist in the family. I will call this method by its own proper name, which is fusion. And by this fusion I understand two things; first, that the ideas of each individual member should be openly expressed, and made the subject of consultation; second, that without going to too great lengths, the parent should strive to conciliate the differences between them, and restore practical and moral unity.

Entire liberty of speech and freedom of expression are, however, requisite, in order that the first condition should be realised. There are people who remain shut up within themselves, from natural disposition or timidity. This class of people make their ideas and thoughts known to no one, and if by chance their affections should come to light, their thoughts are still wrapt up in an impenetrable secret, and hidden by a dense cloud.

Where such dispositions are found, there can be no possible exchange of appreciations and judgments. The ice must be broken, and the fortress taken by storm. But we must be cautious, for it is never by constraint that we shall be able to effect a breach, or see what is going on inside. The walls of which I speak are like those of ancient Jericho; they give way not before the paraphernalia of war, but rather before pacific demonstrations, inspired by sentiments of religion and affection. Even as Joshua and his army went seven times round the walls of Jericho, so must we go seven times round that individual who closes his approaches, and entrenches himself behind them. We must triumph over his delays by patience, and over his apprehensions by accents of sympathy. We must take him, as it were, in a net of tenderness and affection. Besieged in this manner by a confidence which insists without causing irritation, and renews its assaults without striking a blow, he will at last be obliged to open his doors, and we shall find ourselves masters of the situation.

When each individual has laid down his arms and given up his particular views, general peace may ensue. But then comes in a work always delicate, and sometimes exceedingly difficult; we shall now have to make a selection amongst the ideas which had taken possession of these minds. Some are totally refractory—they absolutely reject any fusion —and are not capable of mixing with the rest.

These must be unhesitatingly uprooted and laid aside as one digs up useless and obnoxious weeds from the field they overrun.

This operation itself, necessary though it be, requires much caution. You must beware, in weeding out the tares, of pulling up or loosening the wheat also. You must be careful, in removing the evil, to deal gently with the organ affected by it, and not, by carelessness, to inflict a cruel wound. The eradication of erroneous and hurtful opinions in the mind of a child or youth is rather a work of persuasion than of force.

The earlier you begin, the less will be the resistance; but when unknown to you, and in spite of your efforts, some few of the bitter roots mentioned by St. Paul have sprung up in the dark, and brought forth the germ of a prejudice, or fatal error; assuredly, then, there is no hand better than that of the parent to seize and uproot it. I am presuming, of course, that the head of the family will be careful to keep within the strict limits of veracity and truth. However enlightened he may be, he must guard against personal infallibility, and know how to mistrust his decisions, to question his opinions, to rectify his errors, and, above all, not to attribute to himself a sort of universal science, or intermeddle in things beyond his sphere. It is only when he is treading on sure ground, that he should stand firm, and advance without hesitation. His convictions will then become, by reason of the elevated position they occupy, like the beacon towards which wavering opinions, and ideas without compass or precise definitions, will be directed.

Unanimity of opinion is especially necessary in the all-important question of education! Very frequently it happens that education fails because those entrusted with it seek severally to follow out their own individual system. This system may be either severe or indulgent, but it is a system based upon pre-conceived notions, as to the advantage of this or that particular line of action, ill-founded fears and fanciful hopes. A man will cling to his own opinions though experience does not justify them; he will yield nothing to reason, or for the sake of peace, and even when the most deplorable results ensue, he cannot make up his mind to sacrifice them.

Education in this way becomes a contradictory work, in which two wills are contending for the mastery, and these two influences neutralise each other. Like in the fable of Penelope, it is a work ever commencing and never advancing, because of the two hands which are employed, one immediately destroys what the other attempts to accomplish.

Divided authority becomes very soon contemptible. The child which is bandied about in opposite directions and left to itself between two systems which annihilate each other, grows up hap-hazard, and in the end is guided by no rule but his own passions and caprices. This is not the right place, however, to consider the melancholy portrait of a formation which has come to nothing, and of an education become impracticable. If contradiction is ever disastrous, it is especially so in this case, and if ever a mutual understanding between individual minds is not only desirable but positively necessary, it is doubtless so in the case of education and the bringing up of the young. In conclusion, think of that model family which the consideration of these matters seems to call to our remembrance. It is Mary and Joseph so beautifully drawn together and attached to one another by the tie of sacred virginity, that you should take as your model, and pray for the removal of all dissension and the perfect unity of thought. Blessed indeed is the house formed upon this pattern; blessed indeed the couple who, taking for the basis of their mutual affection this holy and heavenly love, can also raise their minds to be in unison with those who stood around the cradle of the infant Saviour in the manger of Bethlehem.

The Incarnate Word is the key to seek for; it gives the normal note, the fundamental chord, the very essence of true harmony. As every note that is out of tune is false, so every opinion finding itself in discord with the Divine Canticle, is by that fact itself in contradiction to truth. It is necessary to be on the alert to detect the first sound of discord, and to be ready to set it right without delay. The living instruments which God has placed in the family, will then form a delicious concert, prelude of that to which we are invited, and in which the angels will join their melody, when they and we shall form but one immortal family above.

THIRD CONFERENCE.

UNITY OF IDEAS IN THE FAMILY—THE OBSTACLES TO THIS UNITY.

HAVING now thoroughly considered the importance of peace and concord in the family circle, the happiness and tranquillity of life which is dependent upon it will follow in due course. When the early Christians gave to the world (what has never been known since) the spectacle of one immense family having but one heart and one soul, *cor unum anima una,* it was because they had one faith, and because every tongue united in the confession of the same Christian belief. There is no necessity for a minute and rigid uniformity in matters of small detail, that forbids diversity of opinion on matters of open question, and wishes to shape every idea in the same mould, and reduce every mind to a strict equality of measure. This unity is not, and cannot be, obtained by a spirit of dictation which carries everything its own way, or by an indifference which suffers itself to be superseded, but on the contrary, by an enlightened solicitude which, imitating the Author of Divine Providence, treats with due reverence the freedom of minds whom it leads by the paths of persuasion to conformity with the light. It must be a true and comprehensive unity in which all are content and unrestrained, a unity which resembles the Church, and which St. Augustine has well defined in these words: "*In dubiis libertas in necessariis unitas,*" "unity in what is essential, liberty in what is doubtful." This unity in the family becomes daily more and more rare. What is the cause of this, and where must we seek for the true reason?

I.

The first obstacle to complete unity in the family is a total difference of antecedents and a variety of traditions which are contradictory. The family is in point of fact, formed from the outset of elements which are foreign to each other and at times even heterogeneous. Two branches taken from different trees are suddenly brought together, closely united in inseparable bonds and grafted upon the same stem. Each one of necessity brings with it its own sap, its own natural dispositions, affinities and tendencies, whether original or acquired. There may even be in the one an entire absence of what gives life to the other. The question of fortune, rank and social fitness, are frequently the only points considered with reference to marriage, and the thought of associating not only natures, but also habits and principles perfectly at variance with each other, is not regarded as sufficient to make the step a matter of serious consideration.

Here then we see two characters united together whose minds do not possess the same properties, or reflect the same colour. It will be with them as with certain rivers, whose waters though flowing in the same bed never intermingle, but continue each their own course and preserve each their own individuality. Their two minds have been merely associated together instead of being united, and this because of their mutual divergencies. On all vital questions contradictions will arise which it will be impossible to reconcile; antagonisms in thought and belief relating to the most sacred matters difficult to surmount, because on both sides they result from traditional sources and from the early reminiscences of childhood in communication with the realities of life.

That critical period during which indelible convictions are generally formed, has in each case produced totally different results; the divergency has been steadily increasing till dissimilarity is attained in almost everything, and these two individuals brought together by chance are expected to suit each other, to blend into one, and to become equally identified in mind and body. Even if a complete union should be effected, it will probably be at the cost of what is most precious to the weakest party, I mean its religious practices or its religious belief. There can be no doubt that this state of things gives rise to much strife, and causes much suffering. Let us suppose that thanks to mutual concessions the first years have passed without any difficulty, still the solemn hour arrives in which the new family is developed, to which it must also communicate its form, imprint its seal, and in a word, perpetuate its tradition in the children God has given it. At this period the want of unity is sadly felt, for the work is unable to succeed without the concurrence and concerted action of all parties concerned in it. When these are at variance what will become of it? And how will it be completed if the ideas that prevail are antagonistic and for ever trying to supplant one another.

It is a very easy matter to emblazon a shield. It takes no time to blend together in one escutcheon the arms and attributes of two families who are forming an alliance. But it is not so easy to blend together opposite principles, and therefore the work of education often ends in complete failure. The child perchance when young experiences nought but examples of faith, of enlightened religion, of solid piety; good and salutary influences of which he receives the impression and reflects for a time the bright light. But as he grows older he begins to perceive that there is a contrast between those who are placed over him, and that the practice of one parent does not bear out the teaching of the other. On the one side he finds no prayer, no worship, no God; the eye never turned upwards toward heaven, and all thought and anxiety directed towards the well-being and enjoyment of this world; on the other, the complete reverse, but possibly except on matters of religion, a voice more sympathetic, maxims more in harmony with the innate instinct of pleasure, and horizons more smiling to the spirit of independence, and the first aspirations of rising passions. On both sides, however, there is equal fervour of affection, and equal demonstration of devotion and tenderness. What choice will the youth make between such opposite paths and such divergent authorities? What choice between two courses, each containing something that affects him? In childhood he no doubt follows the footsteps of his mother, but the time comes when he will probably begin to follow those of his father, and also possibly of some of those ancestors of his whose lives are placed before him as excellent models. It is a terrible temptation for a young man, especially at the time of life when the voice of nature speaks with loudest voice, and when a kind of unknown fermentation is felt going on within him.

The Almighty, whom the teaching of one parent has revealed to him, is, no doubt, a God of love, but also One Who will ask sacrifices of him.

How much more fascinating and seductive is that broad and flowery path, trodden, without thought of Heaven, by some of those to whom he owes obedience and respect, especially when he may have caught more than once, from their unguarded lips, words of indifference, or the smile and sneer of scepticism.

His choice is soon made. God grant it may, if wrong in the first instance, not be decisive.

The family has exercised upon the child a part only of the religious influence it owed him, and it will soon become evident that this mutilated action is insufficient and even useless. The daily phenomenon of Nature is enough to demonstrate this.

See the luminous rays of light that the sun sends us, which are distinguished for their remarkable unity, and yet the greater number of objects they reach, possess an elective power which severs and divides them. Some rays are absorbed, and some reflected, as if this choice were made according to the character which was more or less sympathetic to the surface they come in contact with.

Even so will the family, an ill-assorted and incoherent assemblage, be analysed and divided by the mind of the child and of the youth. Interested in getting rid of restraint which is irksome, and in preserving only what is pleasant, he will too quickly finish by rejecting the practice of Christian belief and morality, and retain only those obscure influences which produce uncertainty, or at least exonerate him from every difficult undertaking.

II.

Beside the diversity of traditions, unity finds an obstacle also in the variety of personal dispositions. Each individual has his own way of looking at things. Every one does not see matters in the same light, from the same aspect, or in the same manner. There are the short-sighted in the intellectual order, who only see things when they are near; others, on the contrary, who see great distances, and often double, and do not always know how to correct their error. Others have a prism, through which every ray of light passes before reaching their eyes; and it would be difficult to say with how many strange colours objects present themselves to them, and in what proportion they change their truth and shape.

The same causes are far from producing in every person the same effects; in the region of impressions especially, subjective conditions are often the most decisive, and nothing is more true than the old adage: "*Quidquid recipitur recipitur ad modum recipientis,*" which signifies that in every action, we must consider not only the force which comes to play, but also far more the disposition of the person upon whom it is exercised. It ensues from this that men are divided in opinion upon every subject. They regard the same thing from different points of view, and if asked the reason, strange contradictions will generally be made manifest in their accounts.

Thus are men made. Thus are made even those who are to live together, and to have only one common thought, as they have only one common interest.

Setting aside the tendency—natural to many—of contradiction, which increases in proportion as two people are thrown together, union begets a monotony which causes discontent, and then comes a struggle for freedom and independence. The youth, and even the young child, willingly sets up in opposition to the parental authority, begins to enjoy contradiction, and to believe in his own individuality from the day on which he ventures to have an opinion of his own. Assent from the lips of the parent brings forth, spontaneously, dissent from his. The unbounded confidence that springs from love will alone be able to assert itself against this natural tendency to opposition, which comes with our earliest years.

This instinct is often complicated by a thousand petty secret passions, which even the strength of family affection does not always succeed in excluding. It may be a feeling of envy provoked by certain preferences, whether real or only apparent; it may be only a kind of dislike or partial objection for some fault or quality as that of defect in manners or speech in some person that is loved.

Selfishness in each case comes in, and susceptibility, which is generally inseparable from it, is not long in holding forth a helping hand.

A coldness, though but slight at the outset, soon brings in its train some secret sore, which the most insignificant circumstance will open, and which the interview of daily life will tend to aggravate.

A systematic opposition follows in the range of ideas, because the struggles arising from this head often have their primary source elsewhere. People are divided in opinions to-day, because yesterday, a word or an expression of countenance produced a painful impression on them; and if the remedy is not immediately forthcoming, perchance rival and slightly hostile parties may be formed. The family may even have sunk so low as to exhibit to the world the sad spectacle of interior schism, of which examples are to be found even under the roofs of the Patriarchs. The wounded self-love of the sons of Jacob could not forgive a younger brother for acts which only too evidently showed the father's preference for him; it caused a profound aversion, and prevented them from speaking to him in any accents but those which gave expression to angry feeling. "*Oderant eum nec poterant ei quidquam pacifici loqui:*" "They hated him, and were unable to speak peacefully to him."*

Domestic society, attacked by such an evil, cannot fail to be impaired by it. It resembles invalids who have a vital organ affected, or persons who, though generally healthy, have a weak point in their constitutions, and whose bodies are subject to some peculiar infirmity. The member affected cannot perform any function without experiencing acute suffering. Whereas harmony and joy should be the predominating condition of home-life, there is nothing but perpetual commotion. Certain subjects cannot be mentioned, save at the risk of quarrels, and silence is found the only safeguard.

But this very silence will be a burden, and will be as much a cause for anxiety as the silence of a citadel carefully closed, wherein arms and ammuni-

* Gen. xxxvii. 4.

tion have been collected, and which is ever exposed to attack.

Minds are in a perpetual state of mutual distrust. Why should they not lay down their arms in earnest, and sign a peace which is indispensable to their happiness?

Of what importance, after all, are the differences of character? of what importance a diversity of ideas upon certain points of detail. If union were possible alone in minds that coincided in every detail, it could never exist at all. Those who are of one mind in essentials can well dispense with certain accessories. If, for instance, the father wishes to see the peace of the house undisturbed, he must, while requiring submission and respect, sometimes suffer himself to be contradicted. He must, whilst forming the minds of his children, avoid in any way depriving them of their personality; he must be careful to give vent to their feelings, and to be circumspect in his conduct towards those he is training for the battle of life.

The father must act like the engine-driver who, by a judicious management of steam, is able to keep the engine completely under his control; otherwise the compression itself would cause an explosion; and the greater had been the restraint exercised on the liberty of ideas, the more fatal and productive of disaster would be the final and inevitable outburst.

III.

Next in order, must be pointed out those obstacles from outside, which, varied and numerous though they be, can be classed under one head, namely, that of pernicious influences in conception and principle. In this category let us first consider the influence exercised by literature.

It is scarcely necessary to remind you that the Press nowadays is a broad path, in which a variety of systems and theories come into collision. There, to a greater extent than elsewhere, honesty and justice are thrown into the background. With the exception of a few right and true ideas, which strive to hold their own on the great platform of public opinion, it is not truth, but the opposite, that finds favour, and oftentimes untruth, clothed in the guise of a teacher: untruth seducing the multitude by flattering promises, fascinating them by its impostures, and giving as remedies the most active poisons and deleterious medicines.

All who are able to read, go through life exposed to an infinite number of temptations on this head. Children, in their turn, run the same risk, and it is dangerous to allow them too much latitude, without guidance and supervision.

Generally speaking, good literature, modest in expression and sure of the beneficial influence it is capable of exercising, does not seek to gain cheap triumphs, nor allure people by obtruding itself on the public notice. Bad literature, on the contrary, loves to create a commotion, and sound aloud its own trumpet, which never fails to secure the applause of the weak-minded majority.

By reason of its being bad, it excites a morbid curiosity, and gives rise to a wish to know something about it, if only to keep pace with the general public, and to be able to follow the conversations that are in vogue.

Parents rightly object to the society of a young man imbued with false principles, and brought up at the school of unbelief, for their sons; but ought they not also to dread this other company, more fatal because it is more persevering? ought they to deem less objectionable a silent intercourse of irreligion and immoral books, which afford occupation for hours.

Will they not find it an unequal game carried on between a simplicity that has no defence and a sophism provided with every artifice; between a modesty that is ingenuous, and a vice that is disguised with every kind of charm?

There can be no doubt that this close contact will be disastrous, and in some cases may suffice to inflict a deadly wound. The mind will come forth with a shaken faith, an attachment less strong and less firm to the principles and traditions of family; with an undefined contempt of home life, and a keener attraction towards the pleasures of the world; with the germs of a dream; with an imagination calculated to conjure up a thousand fantastic pictures, which will transform themselves into a thousand temptations. Even men of age and experience, though more solid and more mature, have, alas! sometimes hard work to hold out against the attacks of anti-religious publications. How, then, can we expect that the innocent and inexperienced should easily escape?

What is true of books, is also true of newspapers, and that to a still greater degree as they become the actual instruments of division in the family.

Men may flatter themselves on the stability of their convictions, and believe in their power of resistance, but the action daily exercised by the Press in their interior life will end in making itself felt.

Unknown to themselves, it will, little by little, exercise its influence on their opinions, and make them imbibe its own. It is like the drop of water which, falling constantly on the same spot, at last makes an indenture in the very hardest marble; or saltpetre, which, percolating through the pores of the damp stone, gradually transforms the whole wall.

The Press exercises so great an influence on the public in general, that it is easy to see what great importance there must be in the choice that is made, and how essential it is to be on the watch against the attacks of such an insidious foe.

Who knows but that the work of unity may be impaired or even compromised by it?

It may be pulling down what you are striving to erect, and attacking what you are defending. It may be tempting and leading to destruction those whom you fancy you are shielding and protecting from all risk of danger. When once a newspaper or pamphlet has crossed a threshold, it is difficult to say how far it may not penetrate. The more it is spoken against, and laid under interdict, the more easily will it make its way, in spite of all care and watchfulness. Children and servants will not see the forbidden fruit so near, without stretching forth a ready hand; and the house which had hitherto been a sojourn of innocence and simplicity, may become, like the garden of Eden, the scene of temptation and ruin.

In this way books or newspapers easily succeed in imparting their ideas.

Now such is the general spirit of the age, that the air we breathe is often saturated with error, and filled with the false ideas and dangerous prejudices which spread over the world.

Expose the strongest constitution to the irresistible though slow action of this medium, and it will gradually be robbed of its strength. The heavy atmosphere filled with vapours, in which it ordinarily lives, spreads a cloud over its face hitherto so bright, truth becomes obscured and seems gradually to fail, Christian principles no longer throw into this troubled mind anything but faint rays of light, which, becoming daily weaker, threaten soon to fade away altogether. What a trial will not this be for the youth whose mind is not definitely settled? Is not the first duty of a parent to know what society his son frequents, to encourage only that of reliable friends, and to keep as far as possible, from a mind still so susceptible to impressions, all that would deform it, or cause it to contract a wrong.

Are parents themselves so inaccessible to these influences, that they can always face them without precaution? Does it not sometimes happen that a man returns to his home so changed as not to be recognised. Those around him clearly see evidence in his sombre and altered demeanour indications of a secret trouble, the impression of which he cannot shake off.

How many a time does such an invisible influence weigh with force upon a family circle, and become destructive of its peace. The hand which is at work is in the shade, but it is only too severely felt in broad daylight, and the blows it inflicts are none the less cruel or incurable because they are not apparent.

It does not always attack the heart; it often only modifies and transforms ideas, which quickly become quite different, and begin to take their tone from outside, being no longer in harmony with the family. The precious and sacred unity in which men should delight is exposed on all sides; it cannot be preserved or even expected to exist without struggles. It is necessary there should be a vigilant eye alive to every peril, a devoted arm ever ready to defend itself, and, above all, an ardent zeal to embrace its cause and make it triumph over its enemies. The first part of the duty of a true Christian parent, is to shelter the family against all external contamination.

He must establish, not only over himself, but also over those confided to his keeping, a strict control and regular supervision, by which he must examine everything that presents itself.

Free exchange and intercourse would, in such a state of things, be fatal. Without too completely severing the communication with the outside world, he should exercise a careful discernment as to what should be admitted and what prohibited. It will be his duty to put a stop to the contraband commerce of dangerous publications and evil companions.

Whether parents like it or not, ideas of all sorts will reach the threshold, and cannot be forcibly dispersed.

If the father wishes a good choice to be made, he must himself hold erect the torch of faith; he must, with the aid of the brightness of the light which the Church has given him, carefully illuminate the mind, and disclose every phantom seeking to hide itself in the darkness therein. The brighter that Truth shines, the more readily will be dispersed these fleeting shadows which cannot keep their ground in its presence.

The great secret by which he can make the entire house a brilliant focus of light, is to be himself its shining centre. Then all the difficulties that might arise would vanish in the serenity of convictions which he will have no wish to keep only for himself.

He must take as the motto of his life those words of the Gospel applied by our Lord to His Precursor Saint John the Baptist: "*Erat lucerna ardens et lucens:*" "He was a burning and a shining light."

The same Saviour said to all: "*Sic luceat lux vestra coram hominibus ut glorificent Patrem vestrum qui in cœlis est:*" "Let your light so shine before men, that they may glorify your Father who is in heaven."

I would add to this, in a more restricted sense,

and in accents still more pressing: Let your teaching and your words, your actions and your conduct, be in the bosom of the family like a radiant centre, whose rays are reflected in every countenance, so that, illuminated by you, all who constitute your household may be of the number of those whom Scripture designates, "*Filii lucis:*" "Children of the light," or, again, "Children of the day, having nothing in common with the night or darkness:" "*Filii diei non noctis neque tenebrarum:*" This will be a sure sign, by which it will be known that they recognise the Almighty as their Father, and honour Him here on earth, with a filial love: "*Ut glorificent Patrem vestrum qui in cœlis est:*" "That they may glorify your Father who is in heaven." This will disclose a beautiful unanimity of mind, a happy omen of what will one day be more admirable and more complete.

FOURTH CONFERENCE.

UNITY OF IDEAS IN THE FAMILY—CONTINUED—THE MEANS TO ATTAIN IT.

The question of unity in the family is one of very great importance, and requires our careful consideration and attention.

As a matter of fact, scarcely a family can be found so homogeneous as not to embrace some members who disagree even on the most weighty questions. This is especially the case in matters of religion, some adopting violent opinions of their own, others having a total absence of all conviction and an indifference for all modes of worship.

Frequently persons of this latter class seek to make public their own prejudices and professions of unbelief, and claim to bring every one else to their own way of thinking, and insist on the adoption of their own theories and problems. Now whatever be the distance that morally separates us from characters of this kind, we are often compelled to come into contact with them.

The ties of blood and the ordinary usages of society, prevent us from being able to avoid them, and a complete separation is impossible without scandal. It may be that certain sacred interests are opposed to such a measure, and yet the frequent intercourse with such characters creates for some a real source of danger.

It shows itself by certain symptoms already manifested, which seem to point to a gradual transformation.

This may happen in the case of a young boy whose mind is very susceptible to the impressions of those around him; or it may happen with a young girl or young woman, who becomes less and less attached to religion, and more and more drawn towards the pleasures of this life, the more she is removed from the society of those who are really pious.

The religious spirit is thus sensibly diminished, faith becomes weaker, and as a consequence, its ultimate destruction may be expected.

The difficulty I am pointing out increases very much when it becomes permanent and habitual.

Many young men protected up to manhood against all that is bad, find themselves suddenly transferred into an unhealthy atmosphere quite different from that which they had hitherto known. The profession which they have entered into and the studies they are pursuing, perhaps provide them only with irreligious language and an openly avowed antipathy to everything that is Christian.

I will not dilate on the moral, or rather immoral aspect of this state of things, I am only now speaking of the evil influence it may exercise on belief.

More than one innocent soul has in this way lost the simplicity of its faith, and even the first principles received from an early religious education.

An attentive and watchful father cannot reflect without alarm upon a situation which it is not always in his power to prevent. Since the young must fight the battle of life, it behoves the father to make them strong and vigorous champions for it.

If it is now more evident than ever that the Christian must be a soldier, it is necessary that he should be early provided with weapons, and taught to understand every manœuvre. The head of the family becomes by force of circumstance a sort of general instructor intrusted with the training of young recruits. He has three special duties to fulfil which we must carefully examine.

I.

The first duty is to sow more deeply in the mind of the young, the seeds of early impressions. In those countries bordered by the sea where every house is exposed to the fury of wind and tempest, the art of construction is carried on in a special manner, deep foundations are laid, heavy and strong piles are put down, and often the different parts of the edifice are bound together with iron.

But should the building be required in the middle of the sea, even precautions such as these would be no longer sufficient; a particular cement will have to be used, a larger and more solid foundation will be required, and enormous blocks of stone must be collected and bound together indissolubly, for it is only thus the waves will be checked in their headlong career, and the storms can pass over without causing destruction.

You fathers who are listening to these discourses must remember that the building of which you are the architects, will not merely be exposed on the shore to the gusts of wind that blow from the depths of the ocean, but that it will have to stand erect in the very midst of the waves, beaten, shaken and submerged in every part like a bulwark against which all the powers of heaven concentrate their forces.

If you desire therefore that the walls should be capable of resistance, you must realise the vastness of the proportions necessary for such foundations. The importance of a religious and moral education was never more necessary than in our own day.

The dangers inherent to human nature no doubt have always existed from the earliest times, but the general tone of society was once towards a belief in Christianity, and though the will was often led astray by what was evil, the mind generally preserved its early convictions and principles. That part which is most threatened now is precisely the basis that supports everything else.

The great principles of authority, duty, religion and virtue, are the four corner-stones which when joined together complete the foundation.

Of these principles, is there one that the radical negations of the present day do not seek to overthrow? A vague scepticism fills the air, penetrates into the innermost parts of the soul, and filters as it were, through the pores of our thoughts to such a degree, that little by little the stability of first impressions is undermined, although they used to appear firm and immovable. And yet instead of strengthening those first foundations, they are not sufficiently well laid, or else left in a deplorable state of weakness.

Authority fearing to assert itself, does not come forward, and duty masking itself, even if it does not give place altogether to pleasure, is thrown into the shade.

Men confine themselves in religious matters only to that which is strictly obligatory, persuading themselves that it would be dangerous to act otherwise as regards the children they have to educate. They are content with an approach to virtue, and often look on things that are the result of passion or caprice as worthy of merit.

Can they ever expect to build on such foundations, or anticipate any chance of durability?

This kind of authority, whilst assuming to itself the work of moulding the character, produces nought but soft and apathetic natures that will take any shape given them, because they are incapable of having one of their own construction. Instead of making men, it only succeeds in perpetuating a race of children, and though impetuosity and excitability will take the place of simplicity and innocence, the spirit of the child will remain, passionate, capricious, and incapable of moderation and discipline; that which was but instinct, turns into passion, and innocent amusements are changed for terrible realities; but now as before, there is absence of reason, an unrestrained courtship of pleasure, and a mind open to every error, and firmly closed against Christian truth.

Such is the sad spectacle given to us by the young man whose first steps have not been guided by religion, or who has learnt to abandon it on the threshold of manhood. If the influence of religion has remained longer with the young girl, God grant it may not merely consist in a superficial state of good impressions, a sort of exterior varnish which may possibly prove deceptive though it retains nothing solid, which if it does not fall when it comes into contact with the world, is at least incapable of preserving her from its most deadly blows. In this work, on which the whole future depends, it is important to make it penetrate further, even into the depths of the soul; otherwise what you are trying to build up will remain suspended in mid air, the mind for ever oscillating in that rough and inconsistent state spoken of by St. Paul, as carried about by every wind of doctrine, "*Tanquam parvuli fluctuantes omni vento doctrinæ.*"

It was precisely to avoid this that our Lord Jesus Christ established in the Church pastors and teachers, and that He instituted in every Christian household a teaching and governing authority, a responsibility which can never be laid aside.

II.

It will not suffice, however, to prepare the child early for resistance. The paternal eye must follow with constant solicitude every phase of his mind during the period wherein he is most exposed to danger.

We will liken it to the solicitude we have about a vessel of war on which we place our hope of success at sea. We spare no pains in constructing it to insure the firmness of its build, we line its sides with impenetrable sheets of iron, we examine it carefully after every voyage and every engagement; and if there should be found a crack, or the sheets of iron should have given way in any part, we immediately repair the damage before further injury shall happen. And yet the risks this vessel will encounter are not to be compared to those awaiting the young, upon a sea infinitely more troubled, and in which the struggles are infinitely more terrible.

How important it is then to watch against any accident, and repair in time the least damage.

The home ought to be the dockyard, to which the vessel can return after the fatigues of the open sea, when it is impaired by the fire of the enemy, and perhaps even half shattered by its bullets.

If there be any eye capable of examining in detail each wound inflicted upon a young mind, it is surely that of the parent. Nature has given him a sagacity peculiar to himself, and also a peculiar sense enabling him to divine the sufferings, the trials, and also the faults and misfortunes of those committed to his direction.

Parents have the advantage of years over their children, they understand therefore the perils, the temptations and the stumbling-blocks which must arise; they have the experience of struggles and perhaps reverses, the necessary knowledge to forewarn those who come after them, and to spare them some sad disasters. God has placed them near the young and innocent, and armed them with a practical wisdom, the result of past years of experience.

Fully acquainted with a condition of things as yet mysterious to early childhood, they become witnesses to the gradual revelation which ensues, they can watch over each phase of life, and see the gradual progression that is made. A word, a sign, a mere contraction of the brow or an expression of face, conveys to them in clear and unmistakable language, secret internal struggles; but even without any exterior symptom, they can divine them by instinct. Whilst taking care not to compromise authority, if they endeavour to become the friends and confidants of their sons, they will find their innocent hearts will open of themselves, and allow them to read their most hidden thoughts.

They will thus see their first troubles, and will have no difficulty in understanding or realising their first trials. The simple and natural relationship that should exist between parents and children, is like a faithful mirror, reflecting the whole mind.

Reserve, unaccustomed coldness, constraint or perplexity, are sure and unequivocal signs. God has willed that this visible providence seated at the domestic hearth, should have the privilege of that invisible providence which governs the world, so that of both it should be truly said: "*Omnia nuda et aperta sunt oculi ejus,*" "everything is open and unveiled before his eye."

Now just as God's providence can prevent the invasion of disorder, and maintain in its place the balance of the world, so also must that of man not be content with a mere recognition of the presence of evil, but must feel that it is bound to provide a remedy.

The parent must be prepared for the very first deviation. It is time for him to step in with his authority when the mind begins to be less firm, when it gives signs of interior restlessness, when it no longer has the same repugnance for false ideas and erroneous theories, when irreligious conversation is indulged in with complacency, and books of bad doctrine are hailed with pleasure. His task is one that requires great tact, and he must specially avoid wounding that natural spirit of independence in the young man that kicks against reproof. Just as a strong horse kicks against the whip and when once started off will not come back even to the hand that caresses it, so will it be with a young man. Such a character cannot be taken by storm; the father must rather study its every approach and possess himself of the knowledge of the roads leading to it in order to get in without violence.

There must be several gates, the keys of which a tender and devoted father cannot fail to have in his possession.

He must await the favourable moment, and must not be afraid should necessity demand it, to lengthen his route and make a digression. He must approach the difficulty, now openly, now indirectly, bringing his own victorious and personal influence to work, and then gently take the wayward disposition by the hand and replace it again in the solid and invulnerable truth of Christian principles and family traditions. If a blank has been created in the imagination, he must fill it up; if there remain a wound in the mind, he must heal it; and when healed, he must repair the defensive and offensive armour, and consider the means wherewith to supply deficiencies.

Happy will be the young man who lives under the roof of such a father; he will be to a great extent free from error, but if perchance he should become its victim, the fault will be that of his own perverse spirit and obstinate disposition.

III.

We know that certain plants exist which draw their nourishment almost exclusively from their foliage. Their roots, if indeed they can be said to possess any at all, are on the surface of the soil. They grow luxuriantly on the barest walls and bleakest rocks, and are not only completely indifferent to locality, but would scarcely perceive the change if they were transplanted.

The case, however, is quite different with those vigorous trees that delight us by their majestic size and abundant foliage; to transplant them without danger it is necessary to impose upon them by transplanting the soil in which they have grown, and from which they have become practically inseparable.

The soil is necessary to them because they are deeply embedded in it and draw from it their life.

Such is precisely the case, or rather such should be the case with each individual member of the family.

In former times when a Christian spirit pervaded

the general atmosphere of society, it was possible that a plant which had not taken deep root, might still have found its own climate elsewhere; but now when almost every wind that blows is laden with deadly poison, it follows that we must more than ever seek in the essentially healthy atmosphere in which Providence originally placed us, the air that is most suitable for us.

It will not be necessary, in order to breathe it, to remain always at home. It will be wafted to us when far away by means of first impressions and old reminiscences.

This pure and vivifying action will come to the young man like a refreshing breeze that nothing can intercept, in the midst of the ardour of passion, the attraction of friends, of business, of pleasure; and it will often be quite sufficient to make him regain the strength he was on the point of losing, and at once recover the courage of virtue and of honour.

This presupposes of course that the roots of his heart and of his life are inseparably embedded in the family. The affections which nature has taken upon itself to establish, are not merely the condition of our choicest joys, but rather the most effectual guarantee of our perseverance in well doing.

The greater and more irresistible has been the

power of attraction towards the home, the more have we reason to hope that at all times and in all places, those who had been united will remember what they once were and be careful of becoming degenerate. The lot of the young man may be cast beyond seas, far away from family and country; and here he may find himself, more than once, face to face with allurements which even the strongest dispositions have not always the power to resist.

An hour may come, after prolonged struggles and many victories, when his strength being nearly exhausted, he will appear like many before him, to be on the brink of giving way. The religious training of early years might then of itself be too weak, but with the truths he had been taught, there would revive at the bottom of his heart the impressions, the recollections, the traditions of old days, the whole crowned with the admirable picture of the head of his family and his virtues.

Can we suppose this remembrance would prove of small avail in the hour of greatest peril? Can we imagine that beautiful picture of the Christian parent rising up before the eyes of the youth ready to yield in the hour of temptation, speaking to him in language that no other tongue could use, and failing to produce effect? Between the inclination to sin and the sin itself, a something which he cannot shake off will arise, such as the recollection of the inheritance of honour he would have to profane, and the memory of the venerated and beloved father whose name he would tarnish. However strong the allurement, it is then repulsed, and the memories and love of home save him.

The strength of this love depends in great measure upon the unity of the family circle; it depends upon the position the father assumes towards those under him, upon the unanimity of thought and feeling he may have succeeded in establishing around him, and upon the mutual confidences that exist among individual members.

Mutual confidence, a tender and respectful friendship, in addition to the natural affection between father and son, and a familiarity kept within bounds (not that which some would fain establish in these days upon the ruin of respect, but one that unites ranks without confounding them), are all means calculated to attract the heart and attach it to the family.

Parents are principally responsible for a result which depends on the sympathies they create, the charm attaching itself to their demeanour and the joy that is experienced in their society. The father should be the secret magnet both to attract and retain the son, and in this mysterious influence which he is called upon to exercise, there is a something which may be said to surpass the industry of tenderness and even the power of nature.

This something is a divine gift to be obtained by prayer, purchased by sacrifice, and merited by purity of life. The chastity of the father is perhaps the thing that contributes most to give him a hold over the souls entrusted to him. With him the avoidance of every stain is not merely a personal question; the more spotless he is, the more does the light of his life shine and reflect itself on the family, the more does the sweet odour of his virtue fill those around him with fragrance and delight; he cannot but be loved because of his own purity of love, his heart remains young and fresh, and in perfect harmony with those innocent affections springing up around him which it is his task to develop.

Independently of any other considerations, I would say to the father who wishes to make himself worthy of the name, and is anxious to unite himself indissolubly with his family, Be chaste. Immense treasures of love are promised beforehand to purity of conjugal life, and the piety which binds together husband and wife, like that which is directed towards God, brings with it both present and future happiness. It is here necessary to consider the question of books which are more or less antagonistic to belief, and which sometimes threaten to impair the unity of ideas in the family, which are spoken of by every one, and which it is almost impossible a young man should be ignorant of.

If they are absolutely forbidden him, the chances are that he will read them in secret.

Would it not be advisable in certain cases for the father to take the initiative, and read with him the dangerous work, unmasking the falsehood, pointing out the errors, and placing by the side of the poison its antidote, so that the reading should become innocuous, and curiosity at the same time be satisfied.

Nothing appears to me more judicious than such a proposition.

It presupposes, indeed, a well-instructed parent; but why should not this always be the case?

The world is full of men who have no leisure, simply because they do not know how to manage their time to the best advantage; others have time which they do not know what to do with, and perhaps make a bad use of. Why should they not follow more closely the studies and occupations of their children, and relearn enough to enable them to find themselves on a level with those whom they have to lead.

I am aware that a uniform standard of literary attainment is not possible to all. The turmoil of business preoccupies some—age and facility are not in all cases similar—but the influence of the parent should not be suffered to diminish or be destroyed by an inferiority real or apparent, either in literary or scientific questions.

Is there not danger that the pride of the child should be over-duly excited when he feels himself habitually in a sphere his parents do not enter?

Will not the intercourse of the home circle be impaired when the interests of the sons are completely at variance with those of the father? I will not exaggerate the danger; it has existed at all times, and has become more unavoidable than ever in the confusion of classes brought about by the principles of socialism. Granting even a difference on the score of intellectual culture, a wise and enlightened father will never allow himself to be indifferent to the moral formations of his children, and will not permit the helm to slip entirely out of his hands.

In this way, by bringing back minds to truth, by taking for his standard the simplicity of Catholic doctrine, by melting, as it were, into one divine mould the thoughts of the whole family, the father, faithful to his duties, will be able to repeat those words of St. Paul: "*Filioli, quos iterum parturio donec formetur Christus in vobis:*" "My little children, of whom I am in labour again, until Christ be formed in you." Galatians iv. 19.

His happiness and ambition will be to form the minds of his children on the words of our Lord revealed to us in the Gospel.

FIFTH CONFERENCE.

UNITY OF AFFECTION IN THE FAMILY: THE CENTRE, POSITION, AND QUALITIES THAT IT SHOULD POSSESS.

It is important to bear in mind that the unity which should be found in the family, as far as ideas are concerned, is not the end in view, but a powerful means towards the end, and an almost certain pledge that it will not stray from it, and that it constitutes the first step that the family must take in order to attain a nearer resemblance to the type and model of the Divine example.

It is doubtless much that peace should be established in the family circle, but still more important that a close understanding should exist amongst the individual members of which it is composed, and that their hearts should beat in unison; but even then we have but reached the normal condition indispensable for common peace and happiness.

A slight failure in this correspondence of sympathies would be enough to cause trouble and sorrow which might prove inconsolable.

It is unnecessary to insist on this fact, because it asserts itself, and speaks like the natural voice of a parent.

If physical unity is the result of nature, moral unity is the result of the intention of nature, and this latter unity is the result of mutual affection.

If the family be really united in its affections, it will contain two special elements, (1) a common centre around which its members will group themselves, and (2) a powerful attraction which will bind them together, at the same time that it makes them gravitate round the centre.

I will only speak now of the first of these elements, so that we may consider the centre of the family and the qualities it should possess.

I.

In every place where unity is revealed, we find amongst the multiplicity of elements a centre and principal point of attraction. Take, for instance, the world, whose magnificence and size excites our wonder and admiration. It appears to us a regulated and harmonious whole, because it has a centre round which the different parts arrange themselves in sympathetic dependence.

For a long time men were persuaded that this central point was the earth on which we dwell; then, giving up that error, they believed it was the sun.

Nowadays science teaches us that that luminary is itself only a subordinate and secondary light, serving to constitute the unity of that particular group called our planetary system, and this, in its turn, is linked to all the others, and probably revolves round another yet more general.

Herein we have a striking resemblance to the family circle.

The family is itself a world, complete but isolated; its interior unity is impossible without the existence of a centre; if the centre be divided, disorder will inevitably ensue, whereas, providing the centre itself be one, it will not be disturbed by a gravitation of a larger range, like that produced by general society.

It is by no means, unfortunately, a rare occurrence for those who are placed at the head of the family (and who should together form its centre), to divide their interests, and, instead of being closely united, to place themselves in rivalry with each other.

In such a case secret jealousies are disclosed by their words and actions, and the two influences being hostile, the result is perpetual warfare. Whether it be by slight disagreements or serious quarrels, the peace of the house will be greatly disturbed, and a relationship which should be full of sweetness and delight will be poisoned; the present will be compromised, and the future, as far as appearances go, still more compromised, for opposition daily increases, according to the law of inevitable progression.

Meanwhile, the least disadvantage that is sure to follow is to make all education impossible. Now, if the centre of the family be united, and also stable and secure, such misfortunes will be avoided.

Let us suppose, for a moment, that the pole of the world should get displaced; can we conceive the universal confusion that would immediately arise?

But without seeking such a far-fetched example, let us suppose merely that the economy of the human frame (one of those principal organs called in medicine nervous centres), should change its position. In such a case, would not suffering and disorder inevitably ensue? Would not anomalies in the vital functions arise? and dangers often impossible to dispel or to prevent follow quickly in succession?

Now, the human family is an organised body, and its life cannot be developed harmoniously unless every member remain in his own place and the central organs fulfil their respective functions.

Should the centre begin to waver—the *vital knot*

to break—would not sufferings and dangers be imminent?

Alas! the hypothesis is not mere imagination. Men do not cease to be men because they are parents; they have often characters that are weak and vulnerable as regards temptation, sensitive and accessible to the contradictions of the most hasty and diversified impressions. If they are not perpetually on their guard, their thoughts, their wishes, and even their hearts may be carried away by storm, and suddenly reconstituted outside the family. Even if there be no scandal, if nothing of this appear externally, and the most perfect order continues to prevail, do you imagine there will be no uneasiness? Do you suppose those minds will be able to escape that secret anguish which ceases not to make its sting felt, even when nothing seems to provoke it?

When the axis that supported the family begins itself to vacillate, a universal shock is experienced, and individual souls lose their support.

They wander hither and thither without any certain guide or central rallying point, and it will be quite a chance if the best feelings of their hearts retain their former convictions.

Herein exists one of the greatest curses of our time.

If we see numbers of homes desolate, and houses

where joy no longer reigns, whose first ardour has been long since quenched by tears, the real reason is doubtless owing to the fact that the head of the family had not sufficiently strengthened himself by prayer against temptation, or fixed his will sufficiently secure on the immovable rock of duty.

How then must he acquire this spirit of consistency and decision of character?

He cannot be sure of himself without being a practical and sincere Christian, relying on the power of the Almighty to rescue him in the hour of peril.

The foundation of this and every other edifice on which he must build is Christ, the crucified Redeemer; it is impossible, as S. Paul says, to substitute any other: "*Fundamentum aliud nemo potest ponere præter id quod positum est, quod est Christus Jesus:*" "Other foundation can no man lay than that which is already laid, the man Christ Jesus." 1 Cor. iii. 11.

Men have frequently attempted, both now and in former times, to establish a different basis for the family, but always without success. Some there are, for instance, who rest it on human love alone. Love is capricious, and quickly changes its objects, and in the event of failure every interest becomes threatened. Others rest it upon a natural sense of morality, honour, integrity, and worldly duty; but these are feeble banners, easily and frequently overthrown by passion, which they cannot always arrest.

I do not wish to depreciate these excellent sentiments, for they are deserving of great praise; but I wish to point out that they are not the true basis for the family. You must indeed gather round your homes love and honour, the feeling of moral obligations and duty; but if you wish these secondary matters to be strong, you must not refuse them the religious consecration which is necessary for them.

Instead of leaving them floating and uncertain, suspended (so to speak) in mid-air, you must see that they rest on Christian principles, in which alone they can find their strength, which would still be needed, even if nothing more than domestic happiness was desired. You who are parents must defend yourselves before you can defend those entrusted to your care.

In watching over the hearts of others, you must also watch over your own.

Of you, as of the ministers of Christ, it may be said, that laden with responsibility as you are, you can scarcely fall without dragging down others along with you. "*Soli non potest peccare.*" You should therefore embrace everything in your affections, and carry your whole house with you in stedfastness, devotion, and sense of duty.

II.

The centre of the family, which is one and fixed, united and immutable, should at the same time be also sympathetic. In fact, if a centre acts upon that which radiates around it, it is on account of the attraction that it exercises.

Such is the law of the material as well as of the moral world.

It was long before this was ascertained in the first case; but it was never able to be disregarded in the second.

Strength, even when concentrated in one point, produces only a fictitious and often temporary unity; whilst intimate sympathy and mutual attraction create a real unity, which is capable of enduring for ever, and become to the different parts of humanity what strength of cohesion is to matter.

If then a moral centre were to lose this power of attraction, it would, *ipso facto*, lose its character and its virtue, and instead of remaining a centre, would merely become an isolated point.

The case is precisely the same with the father of the family.

He must occupy a place apart from everything else. He is the origin of everything, and the centre towards which everything gravitates.

Nature herself has been careful to cause this

upward movement, so as to establish these tendencies and create these sympathies; this is recognised as a general rule, and should be recognised also as a law of Providence.

The Will of God is to do great things by means of instruments which are frequently insignificant.

What more unimportant, for instance, than those powers spread over bodies that science calls infinitesimal matter, because they have their place in the lowest particles of material beings? These infinitesimal powers offer, as a rule, but a feeble and impotent resistance, and yet it is they, collectively, that maintain the balance of worlds. The love a child experiences for its father may appear like one of these small forces, which might easily pass by unnoticed; and yet this love, with that which flows from it, produces and supports all that is greatest in humanity. It constitutes the moral unity of the family as well as that of the nation; it inspires domestic devotion, and carries love of country to heroism. Love of home and love of country are closely allied, and spring from the same source. These two forms of devotion unite in the depths of the soul, and rise in the same breath. Both appertain to that natural and primeval religion which Christianity develops and completes, from which it draws the most beautiful virtues, and with the aid of which it has filled the most magnificent pages of history.

The father, then, is all powerful. It behoves him to seize this power in good time, and prepare it for the great work it must accomplish. Every one of you to whom this task is entrusted, difficult though it be, nature has aided, and bestowed on you a strength engendered without labour, as the effect of spontaneous inclinations: a strength possessed by every father, by reason and in virtue of the position he occupies, and almost independently of his personal qualities.

He possesses, nevertheless, the power of increasing or lessening it.

Doubtless, in the first instance, natural instinct produces affection in the heart of the child; but by degrees this instinct becomes intelligent, and capable of discerning the evil as well as the good.

In the early years of childhood the parents are looked upon as the ideal of perfection.

The child imagines the knowledge of his father has no bounds, and for this reason questions him on every subject, without even suspecting the possibility of his being embarrassed, or at fault for an answer.

In the same way he attributes to his parents every virtue; he thinks he cannot do better than imitate them, for they are to him the living representatives of the good and the beautiful, the idea of which shines in the depth of his conscience. Alas! enlightenment, as it increases, frequently shows him a blemish in those whom Providence has given to him as models; and as he learns to know them better, they gradually descend from the elevated rank on which his love had placed them. This awakening of the young mind is one of the most painful experiences in life, and it is a very serious matter when this disenchantment begins at home.

Enough of melancholy experiences await the young in the outer world, without an intimate acquaintance with the weakness of humanity in the home circle. Children should find in those who guide and surround them one of those sights that elevate and raise the mind; they should be fired with the noble ambition of walking in the paternal footsteps, and treading the path of honour, which is the moral triumph of man over himself.

The more the father harmonises with the character which combines prudence, affection, and firmness, the more sure will he be to preserve and increase the affection of his children.

In the present day we see many heads of families who appear to place themselves in a subordinate position to their children.

It is a strange disregard of parental dignity for fathers to give themselves up to the complete disposal of their sons; to flatter their every desire, perhaps court their passions, and endeavour, by dint of every possible concession, to obtain their friendship and good-will. Such fathers are like sovereigns of weak character, who aim at popularity, but succeed in losing it; because, having neither the energy to insist on what is right, or the courage to repress what is bad, they tolerate every kind of disorder.

Under their rule, authority becomes illusive, and the child soon finds out the best course to pursue in order to obtain what he wishes. He places his favours at a high price, and bestows a smile only as a speculation; his caresses and endearments must be purchased, for it is only when all his wishes are satisfied that he vouchsafes to give the father the benefit of such expressions and affection.

He has both caresses and ill-temper at his disposal, and knowing well that his tears are never resisted, makes use of them to exercise a regular despotism. Such a spirit is nought but the triumph of instinct over reason, the perpetual victory of a will, inconsistent, blind and disordered, over a wisdom and experience which should have prevented and repressed its vagaries. The authority thus abdicated is exercised by a weak and passionate mind, who makes use of it to place every one around him under an insupportable tyranny.

Who has not seen a house where order is reversed,

because the authority which ought to have come from above comes from below? Amongst these weak and uncertain wills one alone asserts itself, and is obeyed; and this one is the more persistently obstinate in its demands, as it is itself fanciful and unreasonable.

The father is no longer feared; on the contrary, he is the one who yields.

The mother, the second source of power, disarmed as she is by his repudiation of authority, either does not dare to utter reprimands and observations which love would render endurable from her mouth, or, if she does venture from time to time to make them, is disregarded. Hereupon a conflict ensues which will turn to the profit of the child's despotism, and this despotism, deriving its strength from the want of mutual concord between those who ought to have directed him, will be intensified, so that if either parent, urged by the voice of conscience or by a strong sense of duty, wishes to take the reins into his hands again, he will soon, from dislike of disturbances and love of peace, be compelled to lay them down.

The child from this time, freed from all control, and full of the wildest notions, will exercise in the house absolute sway. His disposition, from not having been in early years contradicted, will grow up in complete disorder.

A mind and heart unaccustomed for some length of time to submit to the yoke of truth and virtue, frequently remains for ever incapable of submission. Parents forget this when they trifle with the outbursts of early passion, with the impotent attempts of a childish hatred, and with the impetuosity of a desire which has not learned to be controlled, and calmly say, Reason will come with years, and this will produce moderation, peace, and harmony.

Are they ignorant of the elements of ruin that every individual soul brings with it into the world?

Men triumph prudently over the power which inanimate nature places in the hands of industry. They shut up steam in a prison of steel, out of which it can only find its way gradually and by their permission; they remove gunpowder from contact with anything dangerous; they trace out the path and the manner in which it must act, when the time has arrived for displaying its power; and yet they suffer ideas and feelings, which are only waiting to explode when the first opportunity shall arise, to accumulate and gain strength. The tension increases while they slumber, and soon the walls become too weak, and the enclosure too straitened; in one way or another the instruments of war will force for themselves a passage, and all the while it is they themselves who, by unnatural tenderness and inexplicable carelessness, have prepared and determined these irreparable disasters.

If then, you parents whom I am addressing, wish the perilous journey of life to be gone through without catastrophe, you must begin by curbing its motive power. If you wish the struggles in which both the youth and the full-grown man will be engaged not to end in shameful defeat, you must be careful not to allow rising passion to lay hold of weapons that would afterwards be turned against you. You must prevent the child during its early years from getting possession of, or seizing on, living forces, which it will no longer give up, and upon which the future will depend.

The senseless indulgence of many parents, which is so much the fashion in the present day, does not even insure them the affection they seek.

Is the attraction exercised by the centre in a direct ratio with its abandonment of all repression and strictness?

In other words, is the child who is idolised and flattered by its parents more firmly attached and devoted to them than when such is not the case?

Daily experience answers this question better than any argument of mine.

These little tyrants of the domestic hearth very quickly forget their devotees, and use the power that has been given them only to cause their parents deep sorrow.

Like those gods of wood and stone before which the ignorant heathen prostrate themselves, they are deaf to the prayers and supplications of those who strive to reason with them, and witness without emotion the tears of despair that are shed before them, and of which they are themselves the cause.

They count for nothing the affliction and the sorrow that prevails around them, provided they are in full possession of enjoyment, and that they can feed on the fumes of the sacrifices offered up to their shameful passions.

Inebriated by the poisonous nectar which sparkles in their impure goblets, they pay no attention to the mourning of which they are the cause, or the bitter sorrow of which they are the origin. Accustomed from their earliest days to care only for those who flatter them, to see those around them fly to forestall their every wish, they are logical in desiring to continue life as they have begun it, and with some semblance of reason are astonished if their parents should alter their tone and reprove and condemn a line of conduct which they formerly encouraged with approbation and sometimes even with applause.

Nothing is in reality more transient than this sort of affection to a parent.

Family love resembles fine fruits ripened by an autumnal sun: exquisite in taste and flavour as they are, they must, in order to be preserved for any length of time, be removed from the influence of the atmosphere that would soon destroy them.

Certain condiments possess this power of preservation, and by their aid any fruit can be made to retain its qualities intact long after the time assigned for its ordinary existence. So is it with the affections of the human being, even with that sacred love that blossoms upon the stainless stem of pure relationship, that ripens in the benevolent fire of the paternal eye, and in the enclosed garden of the home circle.

It also requires a condiment which is called respect, and without this it has little strength or fragrance.

People imagine they can make the relationship between father and son easier by overthrowing every barrier, and think that the law of equality now in fashion favours confidence, and draws hearts together by obliterating all lines of distinction.

But Providence has arranged what is best, and when men attempt to correct God's work, they only succeed in spoiling it; when in their presumption they imagine they are adding to its arrangements, in reality they are only subtracting from its beauty and perfection.

Nature has endowed the father with superiority of age, prudence, and acquired wisdom, which he must turn to the best account.

The child, in its moral aspect, should be moulded and fashioned by the intelligent hands of the Christian parent, but when an attempt is made to place upon the same footing two beings—one of which must rightly, and almost of necessity, be subordinate to the other, the result is fatal.

As equality introduces itself, the action of the parent decreases, and not only are his rights attacked, but even the affections on which he had counted gradually vanish and disappear.

The law of respect is not a law of repulsion, but, on the contrary, a law of attraction. It is a self-evident truth that nothing can be loved that is not worthy of respect. This is the reason why passions that are conceived independently of this virtue are mere passing sentiments of attraction and impressions, without durability. Even in works of fiction, in order to impart to such passions greater depth, writers must of necessity contrive that they should secure some esteem or some respect; so true is it, that only on this foundation ordinary affection is able to build up a solid construction.

Family affection must have respect for its basis in order that it may stand secure. A noble dignity, free from formality or harshness, which knows how to bend without compromising its position, is more suitable to the father than an ill-regulated familiarity, by which nothing but a sort of schoolboy friendship is obtained. The child then forgets the author of its life, and regards him as nothing more than a companion who affords him recreation—I might almost say, a plaything which amuses him. It is natural to his age to be soon tired both of the plaything and the companion, and when he no longer finds in either any pleasure, he will turn away and seek the attraction of some other novelty.

How much wiser would it be for the father, instead of building his ascendancy on attractions that fade away, to establish it on those that cannot be altered either by time or circumstances.

True and unfailing devotion to the happiness of the family is itself the attraction which possesses most stability.

When the father does not live for himself, but is altogether given up to the happiness of his household, recoils before no difficulty, and refuses no sacrifice, he may rest assured that sooner or later justice will be done him.

The child, as he becomes capable of understanding and begins to reflect, becomes more and more aware of what he owes to the daily and hourly sacrifices of the parent; touched more by the solicitude of this visible providence than by outward caresses, he will become attached to it by indissoluble bonds of affection and gratitude. This providence should, moreover, show itself to him under an aspect pleasing, and calculated to gain his sympathies.

If virtue had to live apart, and as in the time of hermits, to retire into the desert, with no witnesses but rocks and caverns and wild beasts, then it might with impunity assume whatever form it desired, as it would alone be answerable to the Almighty.

But such is not the case when it has to be cultivated in the bosom of society, or has to be the bright crown of the domestic hearth.

In the circle of the family, virtue is neither complete nor well-regulated if it cannot present itself under an aspect of amiability. It is not sufficient that it should be solid, it must also be attractive; it is not sufficient that it should be devoted, unless its devotion has also an attractive character.

It must be able to exercise such discretion that it can prevent any undue excess of austerity, or any exaggerated strictness. Its firmness must be gentle, its severity benevolent, its dignity easy, and its authority yielding.

It must know how to keep its position, and yet share the interests of those under it, with so much love that perfect ease may prevail in its intercourse, and fear and constraint may never be felt.

It is necessary for every kind of authority to make

itself gracious, and this is always easy for the authority exercised by the father, which will gain rather than lose favour, by a faithful performance of its duties.

Firmness coupled with gentleness, instead of diminishing its power of attraction, is rather a necessary condition to it.

The centre of the family in such a case will be united and firmly established, without losing its powers of sympathy.

The type to take as a model is that of Our Lord risen from the dead. He stands in the midst of the adopted family he has taken to Himself, who behold Him again, after the desolation of Calvary, crowned with glory and triumphant over death.

His victory invested Him in the eyes of the long unbelieving disciples with a new authority. But yet observe how He partially hides the majesty of His countenance; how He eclipses and softens the too resplendent rays which start from His countenance; how indulgent and persuasive are His words, even in the administration of rebukes, so that those who have erred make endless reparation in rendering Him a double degree of devotion and love.

Let us contemplate these admirable mysteries, and strive more and more to carry into life, and especially into family life, the privileges of this glorious resurrection. Under the constant action of grace, a progressive transfiguration will take place—the dross will disappear, and everything sepulchral will be cast away.

The head of the family, reinvigorated, and bearing the garment of light, will again assume his rightful position, and be the cause of joy and happiness.

SIXTH CONFERENCE.

UNITY OF AFFECTION IN THE FAMILY (CONTINUED).—
THE BOND THAT UNITES THE MEMBERS TO THE
CENTRE.

IN the last Conference we considered the fundamental conditions necessary for unity amongst the members of the family, and we laid down that two things were necessary for its existence. Firstly, that there should be in the family a living centre, and that that centre should be established on a sure foundation, at unity with itself, and a source of attraction to everything around it. Secondly, that a link should exist attaching the various component parts to the centre.

As yet we have only enunciated this theory, but the time has now arrived to study it in detail, and to ascertain what it involves.

The link which unites the head of the family to its members need not be sought for from afar; nature has taken care to provide it.

It is based upon the very existence of its members, in their origin and identity of blood and life, and in that admirable order of generation by which each individual is the substance and continuation of those who gave him life. Such is the fundamental and providential fact, the necessary and indissoluble bond.

The perpetuation of the human race is based upon this economy, and the family is constituted by the relations that are consequent upon it.

Doubtless the great Creator could have accomplished His end otherwise.

The succession of beings gifted with reason upon earth might have been derived from a cause other than this process of generation. But mankind would then have been nought but a series of detached links, and would not have formed the continuous chain in which it is impossible to find an interruption or a void.

In such a case, that most beautiful of all organisations, the family circle, which we are now considering, could not have existed. The moral and religious harmonies revealing themselves in the family have a hidden root, and this root is wholly buried in one primeval fact: namely, the dependence in which men are placed towards their parents as regards the transmission of life.

Let us consider the issues involved, and let us endeavour to realise the natural link existing between the father and his offspring; for it is our task to impart to it a solidity proof against trial, and a character of lasting durability.

I.

The first tangible phenomenon which ordinarily results from the unity of substance between father and son is physical likeness—a kind of seal imprinted by the hand of nature, as if to mark a property, and to reveal to the world at large from what stock each individual is descended.

As the Divine Maker of life created the first man Adam in His own image and likeness, so do His co-operators act each in his own particular sphere.

Each source engraves its own image upon what comes from it, and this indelible imprint, which often continues through many generations, without alteration, still enables mankind to recognise those belonging to the same stem, even when the ordinary vicissitudes of life have created distances between them.

The same features and characteristics will be found in the most opposite quarters, revealing the original condition, and family likenesses will be discovered which no amount of prosperity or adversity can obliterate. Occasionally they may act as a warning against vice, and from their very existence cause shame and remorse; but more ordinarily they are merely signs which enable the descendants of the same race to fraternize, even when widely separated by social and conventional distinctions.

The vulgar tongue, which generally contains a good deal of philosophy, admirably expresses this truth. In tracing a genealogical descent, it points to a tree (that is to say, a single stem) furnished with branches dividing and subdividing into numberless shoots. The tree, then, is the family, and its leaves and flowers, unlike those of the vegetable order, continuously bear witness to the stamp of their origin.

In ascending the scale of beings, the character of production is more clearly defined, until it reaches in man its most complete expression.

The family may be said to resemble a clever artist who can reproduce at will the same model, without repetition; it has also its type which it diversifies without abandoning; every physiognomy represents it, and yet each is distinguishable from the other, and thus is formed an admirable unity in multiplicity, which God has not established without reason in the physical order, and which must have its counterpart in the moral order also.

It is well known that men not only inherit from their parents certain features, as the cast of a face, but that the natural inheritance which accrues to them extends farther, and contains aptitudes, instincts, and moral dispositions, through which the same law of solidarity, dissemblance, and indefinite variations executed upon the same theme is found. But here a new element comes in, which must also be taken into account, and which has the power of effecting great changes.

In exterior likenesses nature does everything, and even if men wished, they would not be capable of destroying its work.

Moral resemblance on the other hand must be cultivated with extreme care, and watched over with anxious solicitude. It will be no avail for you, parents, to perpetuate in your children a name, a race, a blood more or less generous, if you do not at the same time perpetuate in them traditions of honour, Christian tendencies, habits of virtue and of devotion.

"The strong spring from the strong," says the poet. "*Fortes creantur fortibus.*" The meaning of this is, doubtless, that the merit of our ancestors has in itself an influence to cause courage and intrepidity to be frequently transmitted from father to son; that honour, when once it has penetrated into a house, is preserved more easily, and that a glory acquired by the parents becomes a fruitful stimulant for all around them.

But if indeed this law still exists, what a number of sorrowful exceptions we find.

Formerly there was a good deal of similarity between the father and the son, but now the contrary is generally the case.

The fact of the parent having trodden one path is often a motive for those who are born of him to choose another.

In vain has nature bestowed on them a similarity of temper, character, disposition; the will in revolt acts against this tendency, alters this work, and overthrows and destroys these harmonies.

Ideas come into collision, doctrines cross each other, and opposite aspirations live under the same roof.

It would almost seem as if different ages were compelled to live side by side.

So long as these dissensions are relegated to the regions of pure theory, it is bad, but when they come down from it to carry troubles and confusion into the mind, it is infinitely worse.

The most certain guarantee that family affections can possess, is the wall built up around them by the conformity of views and inclinations.

When the parent has tuned the soul of the child to his own, the two instruments should have a similar sound; but when this is neglected, the notes of one or both are discordant, and the ear is thereby wounded. You parents are the conductors of the orchestra, and it behoves you to take care that your tone be true. This is important, so that the instrument of your children may be regulated by your own.

It often happens, nowadays, that the rising generation pursue an opposite course to that which preceded it: under the same roof may be found two minds determinedly hostile, who can hardly agree upon any subjects, and this because the family has not taken pains to complete the outlines brought to it by nature, or that in filling them in it has gone the wrong way to work. Some people suffer each different character to develop itself at hazard; they have no general ideas in common, no fixed plan, and they can make no efforts to induce opinions and tendencies to form in their union a closely united mass.

And yet it would be possible, without violently bending down the branches, to have put them by gentle means in the right direction, and to have caused them to converge one towards the other; in fact, to have made them ally themselves one to another, and by this very alliance to have imparted to them a new strength. To attain this, unity must necessarily exist between the two heads of the family, and yet these are perhaps divided.

The atmosphere into which the youth is going to be placed, perhaps for many years, should be homogeneous with that out of which he comes; and yet this is very often the contrary.

At a time when the fragile plant is susceptible to new habits, it is uprooted from the soil in which it was nurtured, and constrained to take root under another sky and another climate, where it will have to accustom itself to a new temperature. I am alluding, as you must see, to establishments which are like nurseries where young shrubs are placed; when they are first deposited therein they are but flexible shoots, but when they return to us the stem has become strong and powerful, and has already taken a definite direction.

We do not trouble ourselves as to what sap it will receive during that period! We do not seek to know what waters will fertilize it, nor what wind will put its branches and its leaves in motion.

Parents too often allow things to take their course. They seem to shake off a work of which they will be the first to reap the results, and in which they should have played a principal part. They seem often to imagine that the seal which they had imprinted on the yet tender soul is so deeply engraven on it that nothing can possibly efface it, and yet they should not forget that what was made according to their own likeness can return to them wearing another.

The carelessness with which some parents throw off a responsibility which they consider as a heavy burden is extraordinary, and the way they content themselves with throwing young minds, yet pliable and without consistency, into the mould of a school, without even pausing to consider whether the mould will prove hurtful or beneficial to them, is marvellous. In such a case the family has almost ceased to exist; it is composed of incoherent elements that have found themselves side by side for a time, without solid bonds, and incapable of forming in the future a complete and homogeneous whole.

You may ask me how it is possible to avoid these disasters, and how children can be kept away from external influences that may prove disastrous, since they are compelled to receive the baptism of public education, and go through all the various phases of public life.

I would answer thus: As long as a spring of water is clear and limpid, he who looks at himself in it cannot fail to see therein the perfect reflection of his features.

Now, there is one period in the life of a child in which the transparency of the soul is not troubled, and like a limpid stream. If you look attentively into it, and sit, as it were, constantly before it, your image will be more than reflected, it will be fixed therein: it will imprint and trace itself in its own light; from thenceforth its tastes will be formed in conformity to your own, and thoughts and feelings similar to those you possess will begin to display themselves. However, nothing as yet is consolidated, and you must be careful not to take your eyes off those features which the least breath would alter.

The sculptor who undertakes to model in clay what he is going afterwards to execute in stone or marble, knows full well that his conception, as long as it is contained only in this fragile substance, has as yet no consistency, and he is accordingly careful to preserve it from every shock and dangerous contact.

Children are the conception of man—the best, the most precious of all; but in early age this conception exists only in clay, and is modelled only in sand.

How, then, can it be thrown away at random, without any precautions being taken to preserve it? Oftentimes, alas, it is given into inexperienced, or perhaps even into ill-disposed hands, who will destroy what has been made.

Even if they be experienced, and you are sure of their good intentions, ought you to divest yourselves of interest in the work? Should you not superintend and aid in its execution?

Must you not, for your part as parents, co-operate, so that nothing should be wanting, or nothing alter its character.

Since you are looked up to as patterns and models, your first effort consists in being irreproachable; but this effort over yourselves, so generous and so constant, must be accompanied by another.

It is not sufficient that you should be excellent as individuals: your goodness must radiate around you, and communicate itself to your children; it is not enough that your own light should be luminous, if its brightness in illuminating those young satellites who gravitate around your hearth does not in the end make them shine themselves with a brilliancy entirely their own.

To attract them to you, to impart to them a normal direction depending on yourselves, and which should yet exercise its own free will; to communicate to them a personal line of action, which fits into their own as a general one, not merely by not running counter to it, but rather by going along with it—such is the work of the parent.

It is, I admit, a work fraught with difficulty from the outset; the parent must proceed in its accomplishment with exquisite tact, and make use of a thousand ingenious means to accomplish the end. He must study the character and disposition of his children, and penetrate into the innermost sanctuary which contains the key of every passion and affection. He must not take forcible possession of it, but rather wait until it be placed in his hands; and even when he holds it he must use it discreetly, with a reserve that will not prove hurtful to freedom, and to such an extent as to place no obstacle in the way of his influence, so that, like our Saviour, he may be able to say that he is the messenger of peace.

The affections in their turn will be the object of a vigilance still more attentive, but always benevolent and fatherly.

By dint of passing and repassing by the paths open to him, the parent will at last succeed in imprinting his footsteps so that they can never be effaced.

In this way the resemblance so much to be desired will be preserved and completed, and become the first guarantee of unity in affections.

The second consists in the development of a universal and innate feeling called gratitude towards parents.

II.

Gratitude should exist because life is a good gift, and those who have imparted it to us deserve well of us; for without disregarding the series of infirmities and of sufferings it brings in its train, none can deny that it is the first good of man.

The Christian, less than any other, ought to question this title, since it is the pedestal on which rests his greatest hopes.

Let us cast a glance at nature: in every degree of animated creation we find the same communication and the same transmission of life.

In the inferior races this transmission is but a matter of instinct, and yet it touches man also.

The maternity that we find there, blind though it be, shows itself to be a pattern of tenderness and solicitude.

It is quite true that it soon begins to forget what it clung to, that it becomes a stranger to those young beings that it used to nurture with so much care, and defended at the peril of its life; for one moment at any rate it will have had the honour of vividly representing the providence of God towards the weakest and most insignificant of his creatures. But there is another maternity infinitely more beautiful, embracing also a fraternity, which, though it has nature for its foundation, ascends to the height of the most sublime self-devotion.

With man the transmission of life is also a physical law, but it is above all a work of love, and it presents itself in exceptional conditions, which bestow upon it the merit and the sanction of sacrifice. A long period has to be faced, and much suffering and many dangers have to be encountered.

The husband who is not yet a father cannot realise his first hopes without exposing to danger her who is most dear to him; each day of expectation brings with it the prospective of foreshadowing joy, mingled with a certain amount of sadness; fear and hope alternate, the former increasing in proportion as the time approaches for the fulfilment of the latter.

Even when in actual possession of this beloved object which God has given him, his apprehensions do not cease, but, on the contrary, a long and difficult era is commencing, replete with anxieties, which years may modify, but never completely extinguish. The existence of the child will cost the parents perpetual sacrifices and self-denial. Originally the product of their blood, it has often to be supported by the sweat of their brow and by their tears; they will be obliged to spend their material resources and their moral power to defend and develop it and to raise it to their standard.

It will be the creation of their tender watchfulness, the victory of their toil and daily sacrifices. Such is the decree of Providence, in order to draw closer the bond of mutual fraternity which already exists in the family.

Herein we find the explanation of that long period of incapability, during which the child is dependent on others, and the inferior position it occupies towards the rest of creation.

It is not much that the parents should have given him material existence; the existence that remains to be brought out, or rather to be created in him, is more precious and at the same time more difficult to produce. Whatever sufferings the first production may have caused, the second will be infinitely more painful, and can only be accomplished at the cost of incessant fatigue and continuous watching, which will exact a scrupulous care of every moment, and a devotion showing itself at every juncture.

A deep instinctive feeling imprinted on the heart of each individual teaches the lesson that there is no more sacred duty than that of filial gratitude. It is sad to see these fundamental principles declining day by day, and threatening gradually to disappear altogether from amongst us.

Gratitude towards parents become daily weaker, the sacred obligations contracted towards them are forgotten, called into question, and sometimes even denied.

I have known young men who had the presumption to assert that, after all, the parents had only done their duty in giving them birth, even sometimes adding that they had merely followed natural instinct and sought the gratification of their own pleasure; and when told of the bitterness they had caused their parents, they had the audacity to say that they also were yielding to the inclinations of nature, thus placing on the same level what is most sacred and what is most vile!

Some children, who are in other respects dutiful, can with difficulty conceive that the authors of their life have any right to their eternal gratitude.

Nothing can well be more dangerous than these pernicious maxims.

If ever they should come to gain the ascendancy, the end not only of the family but of the entire human race will be at hand.

If indeed the propagation of the human race is no longer considered save as an act of selfish gratification; if the mother who gives life at the peril of her own, and if the father who sacrifices his rest and his pleasures, are supposed merely to seek for their own personal satisfaction and follow a mere instinct of nature like the brute creation, then may virtue and heroism be said to exist no longer, and what has hitherto been considered an exalted sentiment must be eradicated from the soul.

At this rate, what would our country be but a land in which the chance of our birth had placed us, and whose maternity would be nothing to us, since we did not even respect that other maternity which should have been dearer than life; what would our homes be but the shelter of a few years—cold and desolate dwellings, no longer speaking to the heart, since there was in them no disinterestedness the memory of which we would care to preserve.

We need not discuss this part of the question further; it is unnecessary, from our restricted point of view, to enter into such debased and unnatural ideas, which have only been set afloat in consequence of the general corruption of mankind.

Sentiments of this sort can only spring from those who have known no family ties, and have never experienced the deep and hallowed feelings of a parent, for then they would have both felt and acknowledged that the father is the embodiment of the highest degree of self-sacrifice.

Without doubt, he finds happiness in his labours and sacrifices, but the joy that God imparts to these things takes nought away from their merit, and diminishes in no wise their value, or the right of an acknowledgment of the debt due to Him.

Children have a duty to fulfil towards their parents which is sacred and imprescriptible, and which is not only one of gratitude, but also one of love.

III.

When we speak of the bond which unites the members of the family, the idea that first presents itself is the mutual love planted by nature in their hearts.

The first attribute of this affection is that it should be spontaneous.

Being the result of natural instinct, it rises from itself without any effort, and seems to exist in the child before reflection and even before knowledge. Almost before his eyes discern the light of day his arms seek to press a loving heart, and his lips open of themselves to his mother's kiss.

The heart seems to take the lead over the mind, and the latter is still enveloped in mist, whilst the former has already conceived the ardour of holy affection only to be extinguished with life.

We know how slowly reason develops itself; we know the long night that precedes the dawn, feeble and cloudy, and which is called the age of discernment.

If even then it can be said that reason begins to appear, it requires a number of years before it obtains full possession of its faculties, or of arriving at that degree of lucidity which characterises youth. But such is not the case with the affections: their most remote recollections are often the most vivid, and their first impressions the most vital and most enduring.

What is the reason of this difference? Why has nature granted the advantage to the heart over the mind, and why should it manifest this partiality?

Is it not because human life in its entirety depends more upon affection than upon learning, more upon love than upon knowledge?

It is the affections that make the man, and it is principles and not knowledge that determine him in the path of good or evil.

For this reason, God in his mercy implants from earliest years in the hearts of the young a virgin affection.

Later on, alas! other loves, less legitimate and less pure, will strive to enter. But if the first remain, it will be the best of all preservatives, and will become the shield of virtue and the safeguard of the individual himself.

The first hours of existence in which the mind seems buried in slumber are hours of paramount importance.

Though parents may think that nothing has yet budded forth in the child, he could say to them: "I sleep, but my heart watches." "*Ego dormio, sed cor meum vigilat.*"

Whilst night seems to envelop the soul, there yet burns a flame whose brilliancy steadily increases

—the flame of spontaneous and unconscious love, the first-fruit of the life of the child.

It is most important that this first-fruit should gain strength, and that in "growing" up it should preserve in all its freshness the perfect purity of its origin.

Parents must watch over and encourage these developments with the greatest attention. They must guard with great care that life still frail and delicate, that is destined one day to become an invincible power. This love is like the grain of mustard seed spoken of in the Gospel, a seed scarcely visible, which Providence places in the earth, and which, if it meets with no obstacle, will produce a great tree, under whose branches the birds of the air will take shelter.

Just so the thoughts which live upon heights, and desires with fleeting wings will often seek refuge for many a year under the tree of affection, if it has been duly allowed to develop.

We know the vitality of family affections, and that just as they are spontaneously produced, without the need of man's assistance, so also do they subsist without man having the power to destroy them. I am not speaking of certain exceptions contrary to nature (and God be praised not very often found), so that, far from subverting the general law, they only confirm it.

The general law is, that family affections do not perish.

In many cases, it is true, they seem to be stifled, and appear as if they were dead, but they reawake just when least expected.

It is only in perverted minds that they give way, for moral corruption penetrates to their roots and prevents their reappearance.

But where these mortal attacks are resisted, family affections are still one of the most living forces, and one of the most powerful means of action, preserved to mankind. There are no wonders they cannot perform, and there is no heroism, whether hidden or disclosed, to which they cannot attain.

Whenever they show themselves strong they obtain ardent sympathies, a fact that explains the popularity attaching to the more or less fabulous types of the pagan world.

This world, notwithstanding the sins of mankind, could sometimes bring forth or invent models of filial piety, of fraternal love, and unalterable fidelity. And whenever such models were found they drew forth from the masses an enthusiastic admiration which was nought but the cry of nature.

So true is it, that everything relating to family affection calls forth a display of feeling, and that the heart of man can never be indifferent to it.

I must here point out a certain inequality which seems almost a want of equilibrium.

The natural tendency of love is to descend rather than to ascend, which in this case produces a certain amount of inequality. Parents give more than they receive; they love more ardently and more intensely than they are loved.

This fact of nature is often the cause of much suffering and anxiety, and gives rise to the reproach so frequently made against the rising generation of indifference.

I certainly have no intention of justifying or even excusing the ingratitude of those children who only bring sorrow to the domestic hearth, and rejoice to escape from the society of their relations as from a disagreeable and obligatory constraint.

I wish still less to diminish in the mind the horror that one feels for the absolute neglect of filial duty so common in the present day.

But in order to dispel illusions, and to prevent cruel disappointments, it is necessary that parents should never forget that it is impossible to instil into their children a tenderness and love equal to their own, and though indeed they have the right to expect a just return of affection, they must never imagine that their devotion and self-sacrifice can meet with an exact equivalent.

They will seldom find in their children an ardour

whose intensity will equal their own. It is because they fail to realise this fact of nature, or, realising it, fail to submit, that they seek for what is impossible, and descend to expedients that are beneath them, and compromise their dignity in order to be more loved.

I have spoken previously of parents who are always at the feet of those whom they ought to command.

I have pointed out that reversal of authority which tries in vain to curry favour by abdicating its position, with the result that the family becomes disabled, education is compromised, the present is the prey to confusion, and the future only offers a vista of disorder.

It is not thus that the bond drawing together those who have to work for each other's happiness can be strengthened.

Family affections cannot be secured by the abnegation of parental authority, any more than they can be secured by force.

It is only by self-denial on your part as parents that you will make others practise it towards you—a self-denial which must be intelligent, and never foolishly given to betray the interests it is anxious to serve. You will obtain all if you know how to exercise parental authority in the complete acceptation of the term. You must exercise tenderness, since nature wills it and the heart demands it, but also authority and firmness, which the future of the family and the interest of the young exact from you; otherwise you will be reproached by your children for the carelessness which had made you shut your eyes to their faults, and which could only result in bringing upon them future misery.

If you want unity to be established in the family, and that it should have some chance of duration, you must give to it, as a prop or stay, the threefold foundations of which I have spoken. You must cultivate, in those who belong to you by blood, that moral likeness of which nature has sown the seeds, and which will bear fruit in redoubled union; you must not allow the feeling of gratitude to be obliterated or weakened, as it is a feeling which forms an essential element of filial piety; and you must endeavour, lastly, that the spontaneous affections by which God has cemented the walls of your home should not only retain their power, but perpetually regain new strength. By such means the building will escape danger; and all its parts being closely joined together in one compact whole, it will preserve for ever the magnificent proportions with which Providence originally endowed it.

SEVENTH CONFERENCE.

UNITY OF AFFECTION IN THE FAMILY (CONTINUED). — NECESSITY OF RELIGION TO PROTECT THEM.

The two principal conditions of unity in the family are a centre, and a physical and moral link binding each part to the centre.

We have spoken of the prerogatives which appertain to the centre, and have also pointed out the principal attributes which characterize the link that brings together its diverse elements.

But nature would work in vain to form a compact whole, spontaneous affections would vainly strive to constitute a homogeneous body, if religion did not co-operate both in the work of the parent and in the instinctive inclination of the heart. It would be difficult, not to say impossible, without this to prevent fatal divisions, or the rise of internal disagreements which would separate those whom Providence had united.

We have previously remarked that God must be the foundation of the family. He is not only the

Author of its origin, but a witness of the contract by virtue of which it exists; and it is his power alone that can impart to the contract its necessary consecration. He is, then, not only a part of the edifice, but the very key-stone of the arch, the corner-stone and foundation of the building; from Him unity depends, and in Him affections must unite if they are ever to remain lasting and indivisible.

This is a fundamental and vital truth. If no higher interest existed, and if religion had not to make people appreciate the promises of a future life, the family would yet be compelled to look to it, if only for the sake of the enjoyment of temporal happiness.

Everything that should exist—virtue, honour, love, and gratitude—would be in a state of perpetual insecurity if Christian piety did not take them under its protection and cover them with its shield.

For the present I do not touch on moral interests, but content myself with discoursing upon the affections, whose life and immortality can only be secure when impregnated with a religious element.

I.

We will begin by recalling to what depth the family had sunk under the ancient sway of pagan morality and pagan practice. It would be impossible to conceive a more deplorable and more complete dissolution.

Not only were principles too difficult to adopt by the unaided assistance of reason disregarded, but the fundamental feelings of nature seemed obliterated from the soul. Woman, being degraded, had lost her position of honour—the name of wife secured to her but a debased and precarious position. The mother, devoid of all feeling, suffered without regret that the fruit of her womb should perish; and the father, armed with the power of life and death over his children, exercised the authority of a despot.

I will not dwell on the details, preferring rather to sum up everything in the words of the Apostle St. Paul, who, when writing to the Romans, declared that he witnessed, under the appearance of civilization and intellectual culture, nought but children in rebellion against their parents, and men without morals, strangers to affection. "*Superbos . . . parentibus non obedientes incompositos . . . . sine affectiones.*" (1 Romans i. 30, 31.)

The vices that had been introduced by paganism amongst the ancient races had penetrated even to the highest circles; and St. Paul, after recounting crimes too horrible to be mentioned here, adds the climax to this dark and gloomy picture by showing the total destruction of affection towards parents that was generally prevalent: "*Parentibus non obedientes . . . sine affectione.*"

Of all institutions that mankind can be successively dispossessed of, the family is the one institution that makes the longest resistance; and when it falls, the disaster is complete and the destruction irretrievable. Such is the spectacle too often witnessed by our missionaries amongst the nations who remain plunged in the horrors of idolatry. Even in the midst of Christianity, what becomes of the feelings most natural to the heart of man when care is not taken to place them under the protecting shield of religion?

Yet the absence of these feelings does not arise from want of precedents, for they existed in the far-off day of infancy, and are identified with the dearest recollections and the deepest and most enduring impressions. They filled with charms those happy years towards which men cannot look back without emotion. They brought them promises of happiness, and initiated them to the sweetest and most consoling relations of life.

How, then, after having guided their steps through these innocent pleasures, can they all of a sudden be eclipsed and extinguished? How is it that such powerful attractions can cease to exercise their influence?

The cause lies in the disposition of the young towards contradiction.

Amongst these dispositions, we find first the love of independence, a passionate and primary love, whose very existence reveals itself from the first hour through the capricious whims that brook no resistance.

It is a recognised fact that a child's instinct is to dictate terms rather than to ask for favours, and that he resorts to supplication only when he has discovered that such is the best way to obtain what he wants.

His first impulse is to thrust aside everything in his way, to possess himself of all that he wants, and to lord it over all that surround him; hence those tears, those frettings, and those cries of impatience that cannot always be soothed, because people fail to realise their object.

Is it strange, then, that the first step in life is an illusion?

The will, already strong, though contained in weak organs, expects to see everything bend before it, but soon learns that it must encounter wills stronger than its own, and has to yield constantly to circumstances that it had not foreseen.

But still the instinct remains, and this instinct grows and develops in proportion as the personal strength increases and the means of realisation become more numerous.

When childhood has given place to the age of discernment, and the senses begin to exercise an influence, the spirit of liberty and independence then becomes great and irresistible. Nowadays, especially—when the current of ideas favours this feeling, when every theory and aspiration of the age tends to excite it—we cannot wonder that the sails are filled with the breath of this wind, which seems to hold out prospects of a favourable journey, and that young hearts are led astray by such flattering allurements and brilliant prospects.

In the presence of such aspirations towards an absolute and unlimited liberty, parents cannot but be more or less of an obstacle.

It is their office to hold the reins of reason, and point out the banner of duty, of virtue, and of honour. From the first moment that the youth strays away from these he will find his father in the way, striving to bring him back, and perhaps forbidding him a passage. Is it, then, a matter of wonder that the child should feel within him the instincts of revolt, and rebel against the hand that seeks to restrain his spirit? His natural sympathies and recollections, as well as his innate tenderness, may represent his parents as objects of devotion and attachment; but at the same time other voices, that speak with louder and more enticing accents, will depict their yoke as unendurable, and persuade him little by little that the time for their authority is gone by.

Which of these two conflicting voices will prevail? If Christian ideas and feelings be absent, a moment will arrive when paternal authority will appear questionable, and the child may then begin to dispute the necessity of obedience, and perhaps even to question and deny any rights of the parent whatever.

The particular point at which he may stop is immaterial; respect will decrease, and this will of itself inflict a terrible and mortal blow on filial love.

Here we find a living power for ever in hostility towards the better part of nature, fighting against tenderness and opposing itself to the growth of love and gratitude, and compromising and stifling the generous dispositions of early years.

II.

Another enemy, more formidable still to family affections, may be found in the thirst for sensual enjoyments which the young soon experience.

Everything—the spring-time of life, with the illusions it cherishes and the imaginations it suggests;

the senses arrived at maturity, which proclaim their emancipation from restraint; the society that becomes almost necessary, but rarely remains untarnished; the world, full of licentiousness and wickedness; the reading of books with an inclination to flatter and seduce—all these unite to increase its power, and together constitute an impetuous whirlwind which it is difficult to contend against. It is like an unruly torrent which carries everything before it, and in which there is no time or strength to resist, or even to pause a moment before the abyss.

God has taken measures to provide against disaster. He places experience and wisdom near the being who is in danger and likely to be corrupted; He bestows upon him a father and mother who are cognizant of the danger, who esteem the price of virtue, and who, we must hope, would prefer death to his moral degradation or ruin.

The work is marked out beforehand. The parents must come to the rescue of this poor barque, agitated by the tempest, and try to seize the helm, or at least exercise some control over it.

But to accomplish this they must often make an attack when it might seem more agreeable to drift along with the current and pretend to ignore what was passing, and float about at the will of the waves.

You parents must not imagine, however, that you can without a struggle suffer the timid and inexperienced oarsman to head the billows and defy the wind and storm. You must not suppose that your admonitions, advice and exhortations will never meet with any resistance.

You must never, through weakness and indecision of character, purposely close your eyes, or, tired out with the contest, abandon it.

The balance which you alone could have maintained being then destroyed, the youth will blindly follow his own desires, and, carried away by their weight, he will gradually roll down the rapid descent, at the imminent danger to himself of perishing and losing for ever all the chaste and pure affections he had hitherto retained.

Sensuality will harden him and supplant his legitimate affections, only to hurl him into connections too bad to be mentioned.

By a continued gratification of the senses, he renders himself incapable of returning to the more elevated standard or being happy in that region where are the sympathies that God Himself has created.

Amongst the many evils of society, none is more sad, or unhappily more common, than this.

The young man who allows himself to be rocked in the arms of sensuality not only loses his virtue, but also the refinement of feeling which he formerly possessed, and in it strips himself of respect for himself and for others, and by degrees the disinterested love of old days gives place to a deep-rooted selfishness.

After a certain number of years spent in mad and licentious follies, which the world too easily excuses and forgives, what will he then be? A degraded being, unfit for any position in social life, worthless as a son, unfit to be a husband or father, a grief and misfortune to those who belong to him, and an object of shame and contempt even to himself.

Is there, then, no remedy, or no means of escape? Will this crisis, so difficult to pass through, leave behind it nought but irreparable ruin?

It is here we see the difference between an education without faith and one in which religion has had its place.

Granting that the former has succeeded in preserving intact the honour and integrity of a young man, and has endowed him with many excellent qualities, these supposed virtues are only the result of inherent nature, and have no solid basis; when the critical moment arises they will be entirely swept away, leaving no ray of hope for the future.

On the other hand, the young man whose early

years bear the stamp of Christian training, though sometimes, alas! also incapable of resisting temptation at the outset, will have a solid foundation to fall back on.

His good resolutions may for a time succumb, and scarcely any traces of them may be left, but there is no cause for alarm; the stem will remain full of strength, which, though hidden in the ground and for a while producing no fruit, preserves intact within itself treasures of vitality and life.

When a calmer period arrives and the young man begins to know himself better—when it is a question of marriage and a condition of life blessed by Christ and the Church—his faith, which seemed dead, revives, principles long dormant recover their strength, and become the leading rule of his existence, and the religious practices of his childhood, which appeared completely forgotten, again come to the surface.

Moreover, a young man educated in truly Christian principles, even in the midst of his backsliding, appreciates (though he will not always pay attention to) the just rebukes and reprimands of his parents.

What a help to parents to feel that their observations, when based on a common belief and family convictions, are sure to exercise a good influence upon their children.

The voice of the father is very powerful when God speaks through it, but weak when it only expresses the frozen accents of reason, and when it can touch no other chord than that of nature, which, it may be, is already itself shaken, and retains little power over the mind.

The conclusion is inevitable: in the face of this terrible enemy, which every head of a family is certain to encounter, the most powerful and most indispensable helpmate, which must be secured, is the strength that religion places at the root of conscience, which will remain long after everything else has disappeared.

III.

The same will be the case with regard to a third obstacle, which generally arises later, but threatens nevertheless to be productive of discord.

The desire of advancement, interest, and love of money often breaks up the unity of a family which had hitherto resisted all obstacles.

The desire of riches is now so great that it frequently becomes a cause of division, when the exclusive aim and object of each individual member of it is his or her own advancement.

As long as the father lives, and his house is the recognised home of all in common, there can presumably be no cause of separation on the score of material well-being; but when the time arrives for a general adjustment, dissensions and differences often ensue.

Money, from being the object of ambition, becomes too often the means of causing great discord.

We know that those who have to build in the midst of the ocean make use of a cement that hardens by contact with the salt water instead of being diluted and dissolved by it.

The prudent father, knowing that generous affections will be compelled to struggle against the invasion of inimical influences, must likewise make use of a cement which will shelter them from all danger.

Religion, not only taught, but practised in the family, will be the true cement of its unity and the safeguard of its durability. In order that this should be lasting, parents must be careful to sow something that is imperishable. Resting upon ideas that Christianity proclaims, and inspired by sentiments of religion, the family will no longer remain dependent upon exterior circumstances, nor be so easily affected by competition or the possibility of conflict.

Human interest will then remain in its own proper sphere, where it can, if necessary, be sustained and defended without the discussions which arise on the subject touching the higher order of affections.

These will grow up to the height that God communicates to the sentiments He inspires, and will become strong with the strength which He imparts to all that he puts His seal upon.

Happily, examples are not wanting to prove the truth of this. There are still amongst us a large number of Christian families whose admirable unity has not suffered from such attacks.

Vainly in such cases does the natural love of independence try to cast out the young man who was undergoing the first trial of liberty. Vainly does the want of enjoyment, and the almost irresistible attraction of empty amusements, attempt the destruction of the union of minds; vainly does personal interest thrust itself between the members of our body to separate them, and make of them a number of hostile and independent atoms.

Family attractions are still triumphant, because they are the handiwork of the Almighty, and because they are blessed and sanctified by practical religion. When these attractions have been established, parents can without fear look forward with peace of mind to the end.

Like Simeon in the New Testament, they will be able to "depart in peace," because they leave in their place a centre which will stand for ever, and be impervious to every calamity—God Himself, Whom all love, and in Whom all hearts meet, until their union is reconstituted and made unalterable in a better life.

EIGHTH CONFERENCE.

UNITY OF FAMILY LIFE.—OBSTACLES.—THE RELATIONS.

A PAGAN jurist once defined marriage in these terms: "A common participation of the entire life, and the undivided possession of divine and human rights." "*Consortium omnis vitæ, divini et humani juris communicatis.*"*

Herein is contained not only the Christian model, but the spontaneous education of the human mind, and the utterance of nature; and yet this unity of life, which was once universally prevalent, seems to become more and more rare in the present day.

This law is the exception, and the normal state is almost a matter of wonder, so seldom is it to be met with in modern society.

It would even seem as if men laboured to contradict it, and that they preferred separation to union.

* Modestinus, lib. i., D. de Nuptiis.

I am not now speaking of ideas, in which there is much opposition and disagreement, nor of the affections, wherein there are unfortunately frequent and important deviations, but merely of the habits, the occupations and distractions that fill up the daily life of men, of the tastes to which they yield, of the sorrows and joys they experience—in a word, of that aggregate of acts and impressions, sufferings and desires, which form so many closely united links, and which make up the whole chain of their existence.

It is to be feared that none of these are experienced in common.

Formerly the family was a tissue composed of one network, every thread of which was bound to the other; nowadays each member weaves his own web, considering it quite immaterial whether it is of the same texture and shade as those around it, or whether it may not shock them by a strange contrast.

The causes are not entirely the fault of individual obstinacy; public morals and public practices, which impose themselves often in such a way that they cannot be thrown off, conspire to destroy the unity of the family.

But the more multiplied the principles of evil, the more incumbent it is to be armed against them, and consequently, also, the more necessary it is to study with care this eminently practical subject, and to regard it from every possible point of view.

I do not propose to enter into any great details, but to point out a few causes that hinder the perfect unity which ought to exist among families.

I.

Business is often supposed to be the first and chief cause for separation. Business is, however, the lot assigned to man by nature, and forced upon him by circumstances.

Whatever his position of life, he is, by virtue of the law, the administrator of the possessions of those under him; he holds in his hands their interests, administers their property, disposes of their goods, and enters into agreements for them in a specified measure. Together with these obligations of a purely domestic character, he has others attached to his position in life, his office, his trade, his profession—important occupations, affecting him not only as a citizen and public character, but also as the guardian of the honour and well-being of the family.

Business, then, instead of being brought forward as an excuse, should be an additional link, since it was the intention of Providence that a certain amount of labour, as a tribute of self-devotion and personal effort, should be contributed by husbands, fathers, and brothers towards the family.

It signifies but little whether the result of these labours is the produce of wealth and importance, or only of that amount of relative comfort that suffices day by day for the household wants; in these unequal positions love is still the same, and if there should be a difference, it is only in favour of the man who can show, not more striking services, but more work and a greater amount of sacrifice.

But unfortunately in our day it is an ordinary occurrence for the head of the family to isolate himself, even in questions of the material interests of others, and to separate his cause, and have secrets from those whom he ought to admit to his confidence and to take under his protection. Instead of aiming at the good of all, he works almost exclusively for his own personal interests, reserving the future to himself, and diverting to his own advantage the stream from which all should have partaken.

He may perhaps squander a considerable part of the revenue over which the law gives him control in questionable transactions, whose dark courses will not admit of a close inspection.

He may perhaps make use of deceit and untruth to hide something that must be kept in the shade, and resort to ruinous loans in order that those around him should not know that his affairs are threatened with destruction. In such cases it will be fortunate if the capital itself remains untouched after the income has been squandered, and if, not content with spending his own money, he does not also squander that which rightly belonged to his wife and children, and of which he was only the guardian and protector.

Let us glance rapidly over this class of faults, in the administration of family matters. They create of necessity an embarrassed and discreditable position, and oblige a man who acts such a part to envelop himself in a perpetual cloak of duplicity, not merely on the world's stage, where dissimulation may be more easily tolerated, but in his own home, and before his own family—in a spot where only truth and confidence should exist, and in the midst of the thousand incidents of daily life, where deception cannot be carried on without an organised system and a constancy worthy of a better cause.

In this way, for instance, a man may allot to himself considerable sums to spend on personal gratifications, which will benefit no one, and which the family is precluded from asking an account of.

We are all ready to condemn this system of iniquitous selfishness amongst the working-classes.

We cannot, without indignation, see their poor mothers, wives, and children deprived of bread, whilst the means which should have proved amply sufficient for their wants is lavished in debauchery.

And yet, in a different way, and under a different aspect, the same kind of injustice is to be found in families of the higher classes.

In one and the same house prodigality and suffering will exist side by side; a lavishness of expenditure that never stops to count the cost of anything, and a poverty which cannot always even meet necessary expenses. We sometimes hear of things that astound us, and of which the world does not dream, such as suffering and privation behind apparent affluence and an external show of wealth.

This may result from an empty pride, a wish to make a greater display than is suitable, but it may also be caused by a cruel abuse of confidence.

The head of the family, whom the law invests with an almost unlimited power, thinking it impossible that he should administer otherwise than with integrity the interests of his family, because conjugal and paternal love seem to form a sufficiently strong guarantee that no supervision is necessary, may himself become the greatest enemy to the prosperity of his house.

Armed as he is with a kind of omnipotent authority, he may use it for the destruction of that which he should have protected, and prove himself an unfaithful administrator. He may escape the judgment of his fellow-men, for they have no hold upon his actions, but he can never escape the judgment of the Almighty Judge of all mankind.

In this case, if we go back to the root of the evil, we shall find that it took its origin in an unnatural separation with reference to material interests.

There is another class, straightforward and upright in all their dealings with the outside world, who wrap themselves up in an impenetrable secret towards the members of their own family. The eye of God alone can penetrate the mysteries of such administration.

Although the law requires the drawing up of certain acts, and the intervention of a public officer, this very personage himself is far from receiving their full confidence, or having the key to their private affairs; no one is initiated, and still less those who have most stake in the matter.

In acting thus, many men think they are acting upon principle, and consider it prudent, as well as just and thoughtful, to pursue such a course. They argue that it is useless to make those near and dear to them participators in cares and troubles of which they might be spared the weight; and to make the difficulty greater for themselves by having to explain their views and projects to minds that are completely ignorant on such matters, to resign themselves to all the trammels and delays of a constitutional form of government, when the concentration of power is a legal privilege, and where personal action would probably be most advantageous.

I am willing to admit, in some special cases, there may be great force in this reasoning. But shall we on that account generalise the system, and disregard the drawbacks, which in most cases are very evident?

The wife that is kept in ignorance of all that concerns the fortunes of the family is like a stranger in her own house—she knows nothing about the present or the future. She is anxious, perhaps, without cause; more probably she is a victim to delusions, and a prey to fanciful hopes; in any case, she lives in a state of humiliating ignorance, and in a painful uncertainty which must inevitably be productive of much suffering.

Moreover, the husband himself fails to have any one who can give him advice or sympathy, and has to bear by himself a responsibility which becomes too weighty, because he refuses to share it with any one else.

Determined to do everything alone, if by chance he should happen to do anything that is imprudent or unfortunate, it is evident that his position will become aggravated by means of this very isolation.

Some husbands and some fathers, to whom self-sacrifice is not wanting, are thereby subjected to moral torture, which they have to bear alone, as they will not confide their troubles to anybody around them.

It may be that an investment, considered safe, does not prove satisfactory, or an expected remittance fails to arrive, and they resort to a loan, in order to cover the deficit and prevent a disclosure; it may be that they are tempted to try the chances of speculating in the Funds, and embark all they possess, and barter for what they have not got; it may even be that they are tempted to make use of the money of others entrusted to their care, which should have been held sacred.

The abyss is thus widening whilst they are trying to hide it, and are always hoping for a change for the better, which never comes.

Meanwhile the family, unaware of the fact, are standing on foundations that are already sapped.

What a terrible awakening if the structure should give way!

The possessor of the fatal secret is eaten with anxieties which he must keep to himself, and under a forced smile there lurks a terrible anguish of mind.

If there had been, from the outset, common action, explanations and sympathy, there might still have been suffering, but the weight of personal responsibility would not have been so great. Do not imagine that you can with impunity deprive yourselves of the mutual consolation and support that should by rights exist in the family circle. It is impossible and contrary to nature.

Suppose, for instance, that the father of the family should be suddenly removed, who will then take his place? who will be able to continue the management of affairs, certainly intricate, and perhaps also embarrassed, and of which no one has any previous knowledge?

If no one on board ship save the helmsman was instructed as to the goal to reach and the course to follow, and this helmsman were to die, danger and trouble would inevitably ensue. In the same way, if men wish that the ship that carries their goods should escape a similar danger, they must never aspire to the questionable dignity of alone directing its course, but seek the assistance of others who may be able to take their place if necessity require it.

Many men think that their wives and mothers ought not to be subjected to cares that may be superfluous!

It is, no doubt, right that men should take upon themselves the greater share of all labours, and endure the chief portion of anxiety and trouble, but nevertheless they must not suppose that it is a way to relieve others from care, to treat them like strangers, or as bereft of all practical knowledge.

However sad may be the truth, they will suffer more from persistent reserve than from any disclosures that may have to be made.

Most people can be taught and gradually initiated in such matters, so that they may be made useful.

It is better to begin early than when it is too late. Parents should initiate their sons in early years, if they do not wish to see them waste their time in idle dreams with regard to their future position, which hinder study, and fetter personal exertion. They should show them by the aid of facts the duty of labour, and the advantage and necessity of embracing a career either to do honour to the expected future, or to supply it, if it should be insufficient. There is no doubt a middle course to pursue, of which the father is alone the competent judge, but he is only an object of pity if the interests confided to him become for him a cause of isolation, and if they raise up a barrier in the family and are the cause of actual separation.

II.

We come now to a second source of evil.

A man may be so absorbed in business as to neglect his family, or, what is a more common occurrence, exterior relationships, like a two-edged sword, may divide and separate him from them.

Each member may have his own individual friends, each his own tastes and ideas, each his own path.

It may be a wife who sees friends whom her husband does not know. It may be a husband who has his own business and avocations to attend to, his study or his club as places of resort.

The business in which he is engaged, or the pleasures in which he indulges, do not leave him leisure for remaining much at home. He may be only seen for a few minutes in the morning and again at night, which is all the sight his family can get of him during the day.

In such a case, the evening should be a time regarded as sacred to the family.

Since they can scarcely ever see each other till then, they should contrive that those still quiet hours should be left to them—hours apparently designed by Providence for this very purpose, when work has ceased, business is silent, and everything seems to invite repose, just as nature envelops itself in silent meditation.

Is not this the best time to meet and enjoy each other's society, to become concentrated in the effusions that mutual confidence promotes, and which constitute the charm of home relationships?

Such is, alas! not the case.

To act thus, would be to reckon without the world, and the world is present, knocking at our door and forcing it, whether we like it or not, to claim the hours it regards as its own possession.

Preparations for a ball, or the theatre, or other entertainments, frequently swallow up the few moments that might have been spent together.

These amusements, carried to any great length, produce alternations of fatigue, excitement, and worry, which will scarcely prove good preparation for the fulfilment of family duties on the morrow.

My intention is not to find fault. I am only pointing out an encroachment of which men are themselves often the first to complain, and when the annual period of gaiety in the large towns begins to approach, numbers of them look forward with a sort of dread to the host of miseries and small annoyances the world is preparing to subject them to, and see in them a prospect of great weariness and much fatigue.

If it was merely a question of intercourse with rational and sensible-minded persons, and people contented themselves with the society of real friends, there would be nothing to condemn: but what attractions, what consolation, can there be in a society that is in fact hollow and frivolous, in official assemblies, in those so-called obligatory parties where people meet and associate together without seeing their friends or making the acquaintance of those by whom they are surrounded?

People say they must go, that custom demands it, and the tyranny of modern conventionality requires it; but this is not sufficient excuse for adopting habits that may very likely become productive of evil.

Formerly the houses of the great were places of resort for drawing together persons of distinction, in the same way that powerful reflectors attract to themselves the rays of light.

An agreeable society which united the most different characters, and often placed side by side the most opposite opinions, was thus formed by means of a combined admixture of clever and distinguished persons. These gatherings, far from being a source of conflict, contributed to the general harmony, and were occasionally the means of toning down extreme opinions; without damage to truth, an exquisite politeness deprived liberty of sharpness or asperity; in short, they caused an interesting exchange of ideas and fruitful commerce of intellects.

Such assemblies were, of course, not free from all danger, but they secured many advantages: they served to refine the mind, to sharpen its wit and vivacity, and they gave to men a polish and social fitness which is the peculiar charm of a gentleman. Nowadays division is the order of the day.

As men have lost the art of conversing, and will not put themselves to any restraint or trouble, union is of necessity broken up, and all hasten to join the circle in which they imagine there is most freedom. In one group may be seen men of mature years supposed to be talking politics and business—would to God that these subjects were the only ones discussed by them! In another, young men supposed to be talking of their various amusements—would to God their conversation was always free from impurity and irreligion! In another group, women and young girls, who, left to themselves, spend their time in the merest frivolities.

All lose by such divisions.

It is not without object that God has placed in man an attraction towards society, nor that He has distributed His gifts diversely amongst His creatures. No individual or collection of individuals is sufficient to itself; it is the corporate body which has life and maintains harmony, and union is more necessary for the maintenance of the balance in moral order than in any other; the diversity of the elements is part of a Providential plan, which can only be realised by this means.

The manners and customs of the present day, instead of respecting this plan, are constantly working to destroy it. They bring division into the world, and separate and disperse what should have been kept together.

Can we, then, wonder that a shock should be felt in the home circle?

There is no consolation to be found in this side of the picture.

The facts I am speaking of are to be regretted and deplored, but we have as yet only reached the commencement.

Do you, then, wish to ascertain what are the real causes of suffering, to examine the symptoms and try to form a problem which will leave no room for delusions?

There are still many morbid principles to consider before we can begin to seek for the remedy, but we will not grudge the time required for an attentive and careful consideration of the subject. The experimental method is often very far from being the shortest, though it is the safest and the most powerful barrier.

But before proceeding with it we will draw a few conclusions which clearly result from the facts just stated.

The two-fold danger manifested in the present day is the separation which makes its way into the family, both on the score of business and acquaintanceships.

Those who wish to avoid as much as possible these two quicksands, must do all in their power to turn what might have been a source of division into a rallying point and link of union.

The occupations proper to man must never be thrown either wholly or in part upon the other sex, always weaker than themselves, and generally quite incompetent in matters of business.

On the other hand, public secrets must not be imprudently revealed on the plea of conjugal affection, or from the pretext of unlimited confidence amongst near relations.

Men should never in any case dispose of secrets that are not their own, nor those that wisdom and justice legally compel them to envelop in silence; but a just and reasonable initiation of their families to their thoughts and opinions, to the administration of business, and the interests which concern it, cannot fail to have a great influence on the unity of home life.

The fact that men have often few thoughts and conceptions in common makes it difficult and almost impossible for them to live together.

Minds influenced by their own ideas do not give them up without a struggle in order to accommodate the ideas of others. This state of things produces a coldness in conversation, and—the very essence of sterility—a manner of talking without interest which becomes quickly wearisome, and from which all hasten to escape, in order that they may seek other companions and other distractions. This is the great cause of family division, since the atmosphere in which we live produces reaction, and causes a further amount of divergency and opposition.

A progressive separation thereupon ensues: associations carry men away and assimilate them to themselves; they give the last stroke to those lines previously existing, and induce in them the habit of placing their enjoyment away from home.

It is a matter of great importance that the family should yield to the exigencies of the world without giving itself entirely up to it. Submerged as it is in the great family of mankind, it cannot have a totally separate existence, it cannot isolate itself, but must take care, in allying itself with the outside world, not to admit of any division in its interior arrangements.

The greater the outward attractions, the stronger must be the inward cohesion, to prevent the component parts from dismemberment.

Certain goods of a secondary order may be sacrificed to the world, but nothing can justify the loss or disregard of those of a higher and more indispensable order.

The unanimity of hearts, the affection of individuals, and the close fusion of their lives, are the great treasures which should take precedence of material prosperity, the most honourable relationships and worldly advantages.

If necessary, everything must be abandoned in order to secure them, and without them the greatest wealth and riches are radically incapable of rendering mankind happy.

NINTH CONFERENCE.

UNITY OF FAMILY LIFE (CONTINUED). — OBSTACLES. — THE TWO FAMILIES.

We have now arrived at a very difficult and important part of our subject, which requires honest and careful consideration.

I wish, if possible, to expose a difficulty which stands in the way of many, and which is frequently sufficient to disturb harmony, and even to render happiness in home life almost impossible.

I have previously compared the family to a stream in which two currents, most dissimilar in their properties, effect a junction.

The two young persons who are about to unite their destinies, not only bring the portions allotted by their parents, but they bring also a quota of ideas already formed, and a mass of traditions and sentiments almost imbibed with their mother's milk. These have now to be blended, or at least rendered capable of co-existence. Were this the only difficulty, it would be great and sometimes almost insurmountable. But in addition to it the families tha have formed them continue to exercise over each a powerful influence, which is unobjectionable when not carried to excess.

As a rule, the more parents have watched over and associated with their children in early life, the happier and better it will be for both hereafter; but however dear they are, they are sometimes the cause of great danger.

The influences of the two families are sometimes at variance, and provoke jealousy and hostility.

It is this species of warfare that we must now consider in order to realise and understand it.

I.

The first difference may arise with regard to religious matters.

On the one side, for instance, Christian principles may be cherished, and Christian practices preserved on the other, the whole code of Christian morality may be disregarded.

Perhaps prejudice may have even succeeded in undermining the mind, and making it distrustful with regard to the sacraments and religious practices. Even if both families are of the same belief, the convictions shared by both may become a cause of division, because of their being diversely interpreted.

Catholicism, when well understood, raises and enlarges the soul, and aims, above all, at uniting it to God by love; promotes a sacred familiarity, and banishes all exaggerated fear from the respect that is due to God.

But Catholicism, under another aspect, when transformed by narrow-minded strictness, makes virtue to consist in abstention, and places the misgivings of servile fear where the gentle and tender expressions of charity should have held sway.

Those who thus interpret the law of God are generally not content with accepting it themselves in this particular form, but try to impose it in the same way on those around them.

Religion, in this case, instead of presenting an amiable and attractive aspect, assumes a severe demeanour, and opens a rough and thorny way, which disconcerts those souls who are accustomed to walk in places that are more smooth.

And if such souls should attempt to claim the liberty of a return to their own paths, they expose themselves to unheard-of criticisms and merciless reproaches. They have daily to listen, through the gloss of transparent allusions, to the blame of what these forbidding minds ironically style an easy devotion and an accommodating belief; whereas it is in reality that which is most reasonable, lawful, and in accordance with the spirit of the Church.

A young husband or wife may thus become constrained, for the sake of peace, to hide a part of the virtuous acts he or she practises; and often the fountain of divine consolations may be poisoned by the bitter remarks to which it is exposed. People should learn to join a careful fulfilment of the law with respect for the liberty of the soul.

God has Himself declared that His ways are not as our ways, nor His thoughts as our thoughts, "*Non sunt viæ meæ vostræ.*" And though His ways are without exception the paths of truth ("*Universæ viæ Domini veritas*"), we cannot be ignorant of the fact that there are several paths, and all are not called to the same.

Why, then, should men assume the right of legislating on matters which our Divine Teacher has left to the discretion of each? Why do they usurp a right to dictate and exercise authority over others which does not belong to them, and pursue an unjust and tyrannical course of moral torture to those around them?

Parents exceed their office when they lay claim to a priesthood other than God has ordained for them; they must beware of encroaching on a sphere which does not belong to them, and learn that their jurisdiction, like that of all earthly princes, expires at the threshold of the holy place where exist the most secret relations between God and the individual soul.

If we leave the sphere of religion, we find many opportunities for the display of antagonistic feelings.

The two families which the new alliance brings in close proximity may belong to opposite parties, whose ideas are not in harmony, and whose traditions and antecedents impel them in contrary directions. The society they frequent, and the papers they read, alike tend to foster and strengthen their differences, so that we see two camps, each having its own sympathies and separate convictions.

Which of the two parties will the young couple embrace?

What course will they pursue?

If they decide openly for the one, they may wound the feelings of the other; and if they try to steer a middle course, the chances are that they displease every one.

Athough some people think it right to marry only in their own set, the generality of persons take a different view, and there is little reason why they should not, when wise and moderate opinions prevail.

Nothing but misfortune can ensue from a mere

anxiety for a brilliant future, such as leads many a young girl to cast her lot for life with a man who is passionate and ill-tempered, who makes his political system his whole creed, and who, from the judgment-seat of his personal infallibility, decides peremptorily, and without appeal, the most intricate questions.

The case is still worse when politics include questions of religion, and touch what is fundamental in civil society. This state of things may produce in the house a spirit of dogmatism that brooks no contradiction, and admits of no doubt as to its rashest assertions.

It may be that the two influences come into collision on purely practical grounds. One party may desire an increase of expenditure, more comforts and luxuries, and a larger household; the other, on the contrary, may incline to reserve, economy, and simplicity. One may love display and the frequenting of noisy society; the other, a quieter and more reserved mode of life. In the one case ambition speaks high, and there is an inclination to push forward and to strive for advancement; in the other, the love of ease prevails, and the thought that the greater the position the greater the responsibility.

Even home relationships and the intercourse of family life are seen in different lights, and questions as to authority, respect, and education, the place for reproofs or rewards, for work or relaxation, are the themes for discussions, which disclose a different starting-point and ideas that are totally at variance.

Between these two ever-active and ever-present powers, each endeavouring to prevail and seeking to assert itself, it is not always an easy matter to retain any special line of action and to preserve independence and individuality.

What line of conduct will be pursued by the young husband at the outset of conjugal life?

What by the young father, who should always be prepared for difficulties?

To what counsels will he lend an ear?

If he attempts to conciliate demands that are incompatible, he will attempt what is impossible; but if he refuses all advice, he will lower himself and become the victim of his own inexperience.

The situation is often very delicate, and one that requires tact, prudence, and practical good sense.

From the fact that opposite traditions and rival influences meet in his house, the head of the family may perceive under his roof germs of division, threatening in a greater or less degree to disturb its peace and unity.

His voice may be neutralized by one hitherto justly venerated, his efforts futile in face of a will stronger and more believed in than his own.

But in order to understand the full force of the

obstacle, it is necessary to go deeper into the subject, and to analyze the thousand and one small passions which find their way into the feelings of the most conscientious. It is only by sounding these hidden depths that young parents will be able to form a just appreciation of the host of difficulties which continually arise, a host truly formidable, over which they must triumph, not by violence, but rather by a spirit of gentle forbearance.

II.

Jealousies of affection are almost unavoidable in the relationship of the parents, and sometimes attain alarming proportions.

There are mothers, for instance, who are never able to forgive the husband (whom they themselves have chosen) for depriving them of a daughter. They regard him as if he had usurped their place, and they appear to regard his wife as a dearly-loved property, which they see gradually drifting away from them.

They imagine it will be lost to them, and they often attempt to take it back by a series of claims which descend to the minutest details, and carry on a perpetual warfare, both openly and secretly, which often exhausts the patience of the husband, and ends in discouraging him, or making him give way.

The woman whose motherly love thus leads her blindly to conspire against her own peace and the happiness of her children is in reality her own enemy.

The same is also the case with the mother who, through a strange contradiction, destroys with one hand what she is endeavouring to erect with the other—who is anxious that the young couple should love each other, and yet is unable to bear the sight of their affection, imagining that she is thereby left out of their mutual confidences.

She consequently whispers distrust, sows the seeds of dissension, and relaxes the sacred bonds, which, thanks to her, may perhaps become severed.

This state of things is not an unfrequent occurrence, nor is it difficult to realise to what excesses it may lead.

Sometimes it creates a hidden disposition scarcely acknowledged by the mother herself, but one that works in secret, and colours her whole life. To what are we to attribute this exaggerated susceptibility and these inexplicable ideas?

Whence comes this sense of loneliness, this despair and jealousy, which nothing can justify, and for which there is no reason?

How is it that no marks of respect and filial deference can succeed in dispelling dark shadows and satisfying exorbitant demands?

The young wife, finding herself, as it were, placed between two sacred duties and two feelings equally necessary, though perhaps not equally strong, is at a loss to know how to act.

She can indeed combine them in her heart without difficulty, but finds it hard to give outward expression to them, so as to satisfy those nearest and dearest to her. Whilst she not unnaturally complains of the unreasonableness of her position, her husband is himself reduced to a condition of perpetual restraint and embarrassment; his words and actions are misinterpreted, and the sight of him brings to mind a train of painful thoughts. He is fortunate if he possesses a house of his own, though even there he may hear the echo of unjust suspicions or unwarranted prejudice.

The case is still worse when the same jealous disposition extends to his other relations. A grandfather or grandmother may, for instance, wish to monopolise the children and to enjoy them as if they were their own special property, to regulate their manner of life and education; and yet all this may arise only from the mist of blinded affection and the prejudice of an improvident devotion.

If the parents of the children remonstrate, the grandparents consider they have been wronged and ill-treated, and that an act of injustice has been done towards them. This frequently gives rise to a series of painful struggles, and sometimes even a final separation.

Side by side with these jealousies, which have their seat principally in the heart, there are others which have their seat in the mind, and cause a rivalry in influence. It is not only affections that are roused, but a domineering spirit, productive of tyranny, that is exhibited.

Thus the young couple find arising outside of their own home one or more ambitious pretensions which aim at obtaining the command.

These pretensions are the more difficult to set aside as they are not devoid of a certain amount of right.

Age, experience, position, the close ties of blood, the legitimate ascendency of parents, all unite in their favour, and seem to confer upon them an undisputed right to proffer their advice, and perhaps, in certain cases, to give utterance to a will which must be obeyed.

Yet it might happen, that in permitting them to increase out of all proportion, the precious jewel of liberty, which the head of the family cannot divest himself of with impunity, would be forfeited.

In thus expressing myself, I am far from wishing to plead the cause of insubordination, or to recommend the forgetfulness of regard, of respect, and of a reasonable submission towards parents.

We shall consider later on the practical solution of the problem; at present I am content with pointing out its difficulties, amongst which must be placed the ardent rivalry and the excessive sensibility which the family has to encounter in its own circle. A contest of jurisdiction may at any moment spring up, manifesting itself in a general sensitiveness and, later on, in dissensions and painful explanations, or worse still, in a studied silence full of secret resentment, and in an increasing coldness, concluding sooner or later in positive disaffection.

I do not think that this is an overdrawn picture. On the contrary, I have endeavoured to keep below the mark, for fear of causing discouragement.

We cannot hide from ourselves the fact that the difficulty is sometimes very grave.

How then are you to avoid it?

What line of action ought you to adopt, as a means of resistance?

Such is the important and decisive question which you parents must practically resolve, if you wish that the peace of your home should not be compromised.

But first let us endeavour to ascertain whether this problem has any theoretical solution.

I do not think it has.

All that we can do is to lay down a few rules and assert a few principles; the rest is so much mixed up with circumstances peculiar to each case, and depends so much upon a thousand little differences, that it seems both foolhardy and useless to try to penetrate into the labyrinth of details.

When once all have been illuminated by the light of a set of general rules, each individual must gather from them what should be his own particular line of action.

Who is the true head of the family?

Where must the centre be placed?

Though we have already discussed this question, it involves issues of such importance, that I feel compelled to return to it.

We are now in a better position to consider the subject in its whole bearing, for we are looking at it from the double aspect of the two families, who may both possess rights of their own.

Above all, it is important to decide whether the centre of the family is fixed or movable.

The partisans of its immutability assert that the true centre round which everything must revolve is the grandfather, who is placed higher in the rank of ascendency. Is he not, they argue, the very origin and source of all the rest. Is he not, relatively at least, the strong stem to which all the new branches are united?

Possessed of an authority which by virtue of its very nature cannot be forfeited, he extends his sovereignty over both father and children, and penetrates through the intermediate degrees into those that are more remote.

The family are, in fact, a continuation of himself, and as such should be shaped according to the law he imposes. Others, on the contrary, argue that the family, though united in its origin, soon becomes subdivided; that different groups are formed, and a new parentage is called into existence, upon which latter rests the immediate responsibility of all that concerns the children given to it by God.

Bound to them by the closest ties, it must fill all the offices appertaining to the living centre, whose influence should be unceasing.

Which of these two opinions is correct?

Though a man at the commencement of family life may entertain the latter, it is more than probable he will incline towards the former when his hair has become white and two generations hail his paternity.

It is quite possible to conciliate both these claims by adjudging to each its due proportion, and by bestowing upon each hierarchical degree its given share of authority and power.

In the world of matter there are positive and relative centres, and there seems to be no reason why such should not be the case with the family.

The positive and absolute centre, the principal star of the constellation of lives attached to and depending upon each other, would be the grandfather, whom all call by the name of father.

To him all hearts should gravitate and all respect converge, and to him all obedience should be rendered.

Men ought to act towards their parents as they would wish their own children to act towards them

If they expect them to exhibit a dutiful submission to themselves, they must be particularly careful to give them a steady example of the same.

But without departing from this original nucleus, it is evident that others exist, and are perpetually formed dependent upon it, and in their turn also exercising an attraction, which, being nearer at hand, is more powerful, and possessed of more immediate influence. It is only by following its lead that the various component parts can be made to retain their sphere.

Such is precisely the case with the solar system.

The sun is the greatest centre; it commands the army of wandering planets to which it imparts light, and yet this does not prevent these planets themselves from having their dependent satellites, which are obedient to the impression they receive from them, revolve round them, and serve them with a sort of deference and respect, without, however, ceasing to be united with them and by them to the universal harmony of worlds.

Such should be more or less the spectacle offered by the family.

The father is a special centre: the group in which he occupies the chief and primary place unites itself to him; it is his office to communicate movement, and to give direction to those for whom he is immediately responsible.

But he himself must not forget that he is a son, and without abdicating the authority invested in him by Providence, must know how to recognise another, to which he for a long time was subject, and which yet retains over him an inalienable right.

If any difficulty should arise in the conciliation of these interests, love will be present to keep back struggles, disarm opposition, and unravel with a kind and skilful hand the complications of wills which might cross and vex each other.

It would be too much to expect that these kindred jurisdictions should never come into collision.

Even in the most perfectly organised piece of mechanism the wheels could not be secured from friction, which would eventually wear out the hardest metal, if it were not for the oil poured upon them, which softens and facilitates their movements.

The government of the family has its own wondrous mechanism, of which Almighty God is the centre, the creator, and the great inventor.

In order that it should work with precision and harmony, the first condition must be fulfilled: that each of the parts of which it is composed should remain in its own place.

Since, then, it is parents who have the most important work to accomplish, they must labour with faithfulness and vigour, and communicate their impulse to those under their authority; but they must never lose sight of the fact that both at their side, and perhaps above them, there are yet other parts whose place they cannot fill, and on whose dependence they must of necessity remain.

Above all, let the oil of a true and deep Christian love flow from the multiplied springs of this piece of mechanism. It is astonishing how much that had seemed impracticable will in this way be made easy.

We have sometimes to deal with susceptible characters, inclined to think that their rights are ignored and their authority compromised, or else that proper respect is not shown towards them.

Age still further intensifies such dispositions.

An impressionable old man easily becomes persuaded that he is being set on one side, and that no heed is taken of his advice; a mother, who has always been adored, will imagine that she is treated with coldness and indifference, and reasoning remains powerless with natures that are only capable of being ruled by their feelings.

You who are young parents must have compassion for these weaknesses. You may perhaps suffer from them, but the persons who entertain them are themselves the real sufferers. When all your good efforts have failed, when both reason and love have proved inefficacious in removing prejudices and dispelling clouds, you must not give way to discouragement, nor, as it sometimes happens, allow yourselves to give up the trial and to abandon to chance the weighty and important interests of which you have charge.

Some men, tired of disputes, abdicate their position, and abandon the reins of guidance, which a wounded self-love was disputing with them. Others, incapable of overcoming the obstacle, separate violently from all that recalls it, and for the sake of avoiding all discussion, fly from the persons who excite them.

Hence ensue divisions and strife in the family circle which sometimes render the meeting of the various members almost impossible.

The world itself is scandalized, and styles such a condition of things a deplorable misfortune.

But although it must be admitted that in some cases they presuppose no fault in the person who is subjected to them, in how many other cases could they not have been prevented by a greater zeal for peace and a greater love of unity and harmony?

Our Lord's words, in the Sermon on the Mount, are, "Blessed are the meek, for they shall inherit the land." "*Beati sunt mites, quoniam ipsi possidebunt terram.*"

If, then, it be true that meekness can conquer the world, it will also insure the possession of hearts in the family.

Meekness, let it be well understood, does not imply weakness, but it excludes all bitterness of spirit, envy and jealousy; it does not preclude a just firmness and decision of character, though it always seasons them with affability and deference; it does not suppose an abdication, but it points out the limits to authority; it makes use of moderation and tender care, and shows how right can assert itself without giving offence, and how individuality may be preserved and yet remain amiable.

The whole secret of domestic happiness lies in the carrying out of this ideal.

Meditate continually in prayer upon these divine words, and try to put them into practice in your relations with those around you.

Take as your motto, "*Beati mites,*" "Blessed are the meek," and then you will be able to implant into the many souls around you those deep and secure foundations which nothing can shake, and which are called by our Blessed Lord, "the inheritance of the earth." "Blessed are the meek, for they shall inherit the land."

TENTH CONFERENCE.

UNITY OF FAMILY LIFE (CONTINUED). — OBSTACLES. — DIVERSITY OF CHARACTERS.

SINCE the moral being of man is composed of many multiplied elements, it is evident that some will not appear on the surface, but remain partially unveiled, whilst others will manifest themselves immediately, and betray themselves without the possibility of dissimulation. The soul has a countenance which it cannot long keep from view, a distinctive appearance and special features which it cannot long conceal. It is, in fact, visible to the outside world, and the revelation of the inner self.

Character does not only result from the dispositions of the soul and of spiritual faculties, but depends much upon the constitution, the nervous system, and the state of the material organisation.

But we are not now treating of an abstract, but of the soul when it dwells in a body, and communicates through its medium with its fellows; we are treating of that sensible compound which is called man—that mixed being in whom the spiritual is joined to the material.

Man is a being whom we see and love, who on the one hand enraptures and attracts us, or on the other repels and irritates us; a creation of a superior order, of which we are constantly complaining, and which we cannot do without, because, whatever be his faults, his society is necessary to us.

Those with whom we come into contact affect us on many sides, but on none so much as on that of character.

The reason lies in the fact of their character being the result of their moral and even their physical dispositions, and the outcome of these divers forces concentrated in themselves.

If these forces are not evenly balanced, an inequality arises, and that which is the most powerful generally determines the nature of the character.

We may, then, with great justice assert that it is the distinctive and most prominent feature of the physiognomy that we have attributed to the soul.

Whether it be vivacity or dulness, gentleness or harshness, courage or timidity, cheerfulness or melancholy, each soul has its own particular note, which forms part of a given scale; but over and above this, each soul has its individual tone, which prevents the same sound from being heard with the same accent.

The general tone can be determined; but what is more difficult to express, or rather, what is impossible fully to define, is the special mode or rhythm proper and peculiar to each individual.

Hence it is that the mere description of a person is never completely satisfactory; hence, also, when we examine the details, two souls never quite resemble each other, any more than two faces.

However, be this as it may, every man is known by his outward physiognomy, according to the words of the great and learned Saint Gregory: "*Per faciem enim unus quisque cognoscitur.*"

In the same way each individual may be known through his character.

It is possible to live for a long time with a good man and not to know the existence of certain virtues and good deeds which his humility is careful to disguise; and it is also possible to live with a bad man and not to know the existence of certain faults which he carefully hides from view; but it is impossible for the character to remain for any length of time concealed.

Whether it be good or bad, it cannot help soon disclosing itself, and the strictest watchfulness will never entirely prevent it from coming to the surface.

The thoughts that pass and repass in the innermost recesses of the soul can of course be kept secret, and feelings can at pleasure remain impenetrable, but it is not so with the character.

I do not mean for a moment to say that this all-important part of our moral being is not capable of experiencing change; that it cannot be improved, transformed, or (to use a Christian phrase) converted. On the contrary, I am going to lay down the foundations of this transformation; the saints show us to what extent perseverance can succeed in producing it, and their example proves the desirability of our undertaking it.

Experience proves that even through these indefinite modifications the character yet remains such that it is rather altered than annihilated.

Our character, such as it is, or such as we have made it, does not long remain hidden in our daily intercourse. Though it be mortified and chastened, it appears at intervals, either in its first form (if the victory gained over it be not complete), or under a new aspect and new features, which render it scarcely recognisable.

Do what we may, as long as we inhabit this earth, the nature we bring into the world will remain; and what we have grace from heaven to accomplish is to cultivate and improve it. Any attempt to destroy it, or change it for another, will be a senseless and impossible undertaking, and will only end in failure and disappointment.

Without going further into the question, it is evident that for those who are called to live together, and particularly for the members of one family, who have so much intercourse with each other, the question of character is a question of vital importance, and contains the key of the problem that we have to solve.

Though opinions may be different and conflicting, it is quite possible to arrive at an understanding, and a certain kind of toleration, which will enable the family to live united and happy.

In spite of differences in tastes and affections, peace may be maintained where there are sacrifices on both sides. But it will inevitably be compromised if characters misunderstand and embitter each other by continuous altercations, and if they cannot be content to lay down their arms on the commencement of any disagreement.

In such a case, though appearances may sometimes be saved, and scandal to the outside world avoided, peace is not really established. The quarrel remains permanent and concealed; and though the world may believe the contrary, there is either a state of siege, or, what is still worse, a dead calm, which shows that the various members have despaired of any mutual understanding, and have sought by isolation and separation to avoid external collision.

It is needless to insist upon the importance of the subject; but I will lay down two principles, from which a great number of consequences may be deduced.

I.

The first principle, occupying the first place of importance, is that no character is of itself radically or originally vicious. This assertion may possibly seem strange, and opposed to generally received notions; it appears to contradict that common-sense opinion expressed in popular phraseology, that "such and such an individual is born with a character inclined to evil." And yet the proposition contains a positive and incontestable truth.

Nothing that is radically evil issues forth from the hands of God; He alone makes natures to differ, and creates character. No doubt in these are found the trace and influence of original sin, but the character being, as we have just said, the result of forces divided over the whole human being, so that not only the soul, but also the organisation and constitution, determine it, it is not surprising to find therein, more than elsewhere, the marks and traces of primitive degradation.

I readily acknowledge that everything impure and unhealthy in the young child is the result of the old Adam, who imparts to every human being the fatal inheritance of original sin; but it is certain that the original devastation, however far it extends, does not corrupt the faculties themselves, or reach their roots; and that the influence it exercises on the character is indirect and reflected, since it acts only in destroying the equilibrium, and in removing the counterpoise that Divine Providence had established from the beginning of all things.

The temptations which ensue, the unbridled instincts which frequently show themselves from the first hour of a child's existence, and are afterwards called by the name of passions, do not deserve, if taken by themselves, and before they have been affected by the deviations of the will, the anathemas usually heaped upon them. They are undoubtedly dangerous, but not absolutely vicious and perverted; such an assertion would be an outrage upon the Divine Creator of mankind.

The burning energies of the soul, gifted with reason and sensibility, may be turned to good, and they will then devote themselves with the same ardour to good that they would have expended in following everything bad.

More than once, when they have been softened by grace and illuminated by the light from above, they have proved themselves most powerful co-operators in the service of virtue, and provided it with resources which it would never have found in a calmer nature and more peaceful temperament.

If, then, such is the case with forces which must be regarded as the least tractable and most difficult of access, such will be still more the case with the general disposition of man, which is not a passion, and which cannot be confounded with concupiscence, but constitutes the special temper of the individual.

That which makes us stigmatise a character as bad, is that we regard it in the fatal development it may have taken, and in the condition it may attain to after an education that has been faulty, wanting in intelligence, and so languid as to be practically incomplete.

We attribute its existing vices to the tendencies with which it came into the world, and thus include everything in a sweeping condemnation; whilst in reality these same tendencies, employed in another direction, would have produced a different result.

The same tree will bear bitter or sweet fruit, according as it is cultivated with more or less skill and intelligence, and according as the grafting it receives be more or less capable of correcting the acidity of its first sap.

We know not the treasures of life that are enclosed

in the undaunted exuberance of the commencement of the human growth.

Doubtless, amongst these new shoots there is much that must be pruned, and much that must be cut off; but there are also a large number of branches that may be made useful and prepared for a future career.

The father, as head of the family, is the gardener and vine-dresser; to him is entrusted the cultivation of the shrub and the management of the vine; to him the duty of exposing to the sun of truth and righteousness those branches already clothing themselves with foliage, and soon, it is to be hoped, to be crowned with flowers. The branch is not always flexible; it has sometimes a force that resists, which will require to be tamed down, but never broken.

To maintain order, it is necessary to make use of bonds which will exercise a preserving and restraining power, without the infliction of any wounds.

Very often the bonds that are fabricated are too weak, and the vivacious faculties of the young, impatient of the law imposed upon them, burst their fetters, and begin to develop a complete state of independence.

But parents must again return to their task, and not allow themselves to be discouraged; should their efforts fail twenty times they must persevere.

for there is no cultivation in which constancy is more necessary than in that of the soul.

Our blessed Lord has frequently urged the importance and duty of perseverance, and promised that it should bear fruit: "*Fructum afferunt in patientiam.*" "They shall bring forth fruit with patience." S. Luke viii. 15.

Every character has its bright side: if it be passionate, the chances are that beneath the spirit of violence there is a good and affectionate disposition; if weak and indolent, that amiability and gentleness will not be wanting; if serious, that there is assurance and stability; if gay, a desire to make life agreeable to others; and if obstinate, it is probable that the sin may only be the wish for an excess of power.

The penetrating sagacity of the head of the family consists in finding out by what loophole different characters can be reached, and what stability can be afforded to the lever about to be set in motion, and also in discovering the elements that should be developed and the germ that should be nurtured and cultivated.

If an early beginning is made, that is to say, before any prejudices are formed, and before any dangerous instincts have assumed a fatal direction in a will not yet rebellious, and in a disposition not yet vitiated, there will be no difficulty in finding, in addition to the corner-stone on which to build, much that will be useful. The ingenuous simplicity of an artless soul furnishes immense resources; the purity of a heart into which vice has not yet entered exercises upon every action immense influence.

What abundance of life is visible in those first desires, that are so easy to direct! What sensibility in those fibres of filial love, which are so easy for a parent to set in motion!

If the first hours are permitted to pass by, the task becomes more difficult; but still, no matter how deeply imbedded be the germ of good beneath the briars and thorns of bad habits, the eye of the parent can discern it.

Moreover, it is the hand of the parent that has the power to grasp and disengage it, and to invigorate it by assiduous cultivation, since it is not really dried up, though it has long remained barren.

But there must be no delay, for the time will soon come when the character will assume its definite form.

The bias contracted in early life is often so powerful, that it is a work of difficulty to destroy it, or to recast it in another mould.

Virtue is in such a case no longer equal to the task, and even sanctity of life is not always successful. The character not only may not have acquired such a degree of beauty and of goodness as it might have done; but may be compromised by a vicious element which has already acquired great preponderance, and which will infallibly be productive of much difficulty and trouble. Man can doubtless be subjected to greater misfortunes, but no misfortunes bring in their train so many sufferings as a character given up to evil.

If parents wish to spare their children and those who live with them a source of continual sorrow, they must seek to develop not only the favourable, but also the weak side of the characters of their children, so as to prepare them for the battle of life.

II.

If it be true that no character is radically and essentially bad, it is true also that every character has its faults and failings, and is liable to external dangers, which dangers are incidental to the direction it follows, and a consequence of the qualities that distinguish it.

In fact, though the diversity in this matter may be said to be almost infinite, all characters are able to be classified under two heads and in two general categories: some are energetic, others indolent; hence the first sin most frequently through excess of strength, whilst the second easily contract the vices proceeding from weakness.

The latter class will be wanting in courage, with no will or constancy of their own, easy to be led astray, impressionable, and susceptible to temptation.

The former will be impetuous, passionate and violent, pushing ardour to audacity, and the love of independence to insubordination and rebellion.

We see, then, that as regards the passions common to both, each individual will display its own special characteristics, with the thousand and one inappreciable shades which language fails to express.

These faults are but the excess of a disposition which in itself does not deserve censure. But here, as everywhere else, excess becomes a vice, because everywhere that which is good possesses order, method, and harmony, and because according to an old adage virtue consists in a certain medium, "*in medio virtus*," from which it cannot depart without becoming corrupted.

Here, again, we have the origin of what is called lack of individuality in certain characters.

It seems as if they were wanting in cohesion, and that the different elements of which they are formed disclose a void.

Can we be surprised at this? Have we ever met with an individual who was faultless, and can we ever expect to see a nature in which everything will reach perfection?

Such a thing is impossible; perfection does not exist in this world. Our blessed Lord was the only absolutely perfect man that ever lived.

All that was made out of nothing is finite, limited, and consequently in some point vulnerable. On earth it can only be a question of degree, and it is because our term of comparison is a restricted ideal that we are not surprised at this deficit.

The truth is, that every nature, though limited, has ordinarily a prominent side; and, as we have just said, it is according to the amount this errs on the side of excess or defect that we are enabled to ascertain the special dangers against which it is necessary to guard. The same law applies to all: there is no person that has not to labour in order to correct and subdue his own character. This is especially the case in family life, because it is a social and common existence, and because no one is exempt from the life-long struggle against self.

Some people, whilst they deny themselves nothing, wish to exact everything from those around them, and while they make no effort themselves, expect their neighbours to do violence to their feelings.

In this way they seek to carry privilege into nature itself, in spite of the radical equality established by Providence, which is strongly opposed to it.

The legitimate order of things must on no account be subverted; the hierarchy of domestic life is sacred, and its rights must be placed out of reach of all interference.

It is never suitable for children to teach those who have given them life; neither is it the place of the wife to dictate as by right to the husband sanctified to her as a guide and protector by the sacrament of marriage. Every one has his own special duty to perform—a duty in no wise depending upon the way in which other persons fulfil theirs.

Mutual contact is profitable to all, provided that he who is in the position of authority himself practises what he expects of those under him, when the very faults that he notices in others become a beacon and a warning either to point out the same faults in himself, or to open his eyes to the contrast exhibited, and show him the contrary error into which he has fallen.

Children are responsible only for themselves, but parents have a double work and double undertaking to accomplish. Whilst the heads of the family have to undertake the formation of those entrusted to them, they must watch with still greater care and circumspection their own characters.

If the divergency of character begins to be productive of harm, and to put an obstacle in the way of family union, they may be certain beforehand that some one of these matters has been neglected.

It is neither reasonable nor desirable for any one to wish to correct everything in other people and nothing in himself.

Some persons cannot brook quickness of temper without themselves giving way to anger and annoyance, and some, of an excessive susceptibility themselves, are surprised at finding around them others of a similar disposition.

Such persons are like the blind mentioned in the Gospels, who are quick to detect a mote in the eye of their neighbour, but slow to perceive the beam in their own—partial and interested judges, who have two weights and two measures, who forgive themselves everything, but are incapable of making allowance or extenuation for anything in those around them.

However good their theories may be, their example is more powerful than their precepts. Their conduct is at variance with their language, and an appeal is made from their reproof to their practice: their acts and professions are set off in contrast to each other. This is one cause of the want of power and vitality in the family circle, and in part the reason why the work of education, in the formation of character, is so often fruitless.

Our Lord did not consider Himself justified in teaching us without having first put in practice that which He intended to ask of us: "*Cœpit facere et docere.*" "He began to do and to teach." Before He formulated His precepts He showed us the force of them by His acts, and thus His life stands forth as the most beautiful and most complete commentary of His gospel teaching.

Would that all of us did the same, and would that our words were corroborated by our acts. Of all the motives which incite us to apply ourselves without intermission to our personal improvement, I know of none that could be more efficacious.

Can there indeed be any stronger encouragement, or any more pressing necessity for such a result, than the knowledge that the efficaciousness of our efforts and of the ministry God confides to us is dependent in a great measure upon our own conduct?

In raising yourselves as parents, you will find that you raise all that surrounds you; and if you wish to make your children generous-hearted, you must follow the example of the eagle who goes before its young and induces them to rise after it: "*Sicut aquila provocans pullos suos ad volandum.*"

In the important question of character, the disposition of the parent is frequently reproduced in the child, and too often to this must be attributed the bitterness of feeling and the chilling coldness which pervades all intimate intercourse in the family circle.

Newly-married persons have much to learn, and an entirely new kind of life to adopt; strangers till marriage, or communicating only by that surface acquaintance which reaches no farther than the exterior, they come by degrees to know each other intimately, and the intercourse of every day mutually initiates them to all the secrets of their moral being.

On such an occasion characters often come into collision; they begin to perceive that they are utterly dissimilar, and that they have different tendencies and opposite natures.

There is no real cause for alarm in such a discovery, and yet it is the herald of misgivings and the commencement of a series of disappointments.

What can be done?

Must not he whose age, authority, and position give him more maturity and more experience set to work and undertake a new education, no longer that of the mind, or even exclusively that of the heart, but that of the entire soul, of its moral being, of its most living energies, of its outward acts, and of its innermost feelings?

Great and admirable enterprise, worthy to tempt

the husband's ambition, even if his happiness were not bound up in it, and magnificent and noble privilege, if he feel within his heart enough tenderness and enough devotion to dedicate himself unreservedly to this work, which is not only a work of love, but also a work of patience!

The teacher will in this way, whilst imparting knowledge to others, instruct himself in the lessons of wisdom, or rather, there would be no teacher and no tribune, but two lives placed parallel, striving in their mutual contact to become more beautiful and more pure, more amiable and more worthy of love and admiration.

At the outset, especially, many ways are open, if both know how to use them, and to find out the quarters that are accessible, so as to profit by a favourable movement. God himself acts with the tenderest care and precaution in this delicate task; He speaks to the two souls in accents of love and gentleness, not demanding everything at once, but using an endless forbearance, fearing to hurt or wound them, respecting their liberty, and only forestalling it by those gentle inspirations which, instead of making use of compulsion, only point out the best direction to follow. When his efforts are rejected, He is not discouraged; when His inspirations are disregarded and despised, He does not despair, but returns at another time under another aspect, with more persuasive arguments and more pressing and tender solicitations, which, though they may sometimes appear to be armed with firmness, are really full of love and gentleness; love is still the dominant note, and one can recognise in it the depth of that charity spoken of by S. Paul in his Epistle to the Corinthians: "*Charitas Dei urget nos.*" "The love of God constraineth us." 2 Cor. v. 14.

The Christian husband, with respect to her whom he has taken to himself, should be like the living incarnation of grace, bearing a human countenance, but speaking the language of affection.

He must of necessity be the guardian of her chastity, the protector of her virtue, the defender of her weakness.

He must be the instrument of good, the model of honour, the providential force which God has instituted to watch, to shelter and to protect her.

If, then, he is desirous of completely fulfilling the mission he has received, he must exercise the same protection within as without. He may be compelled to struggle against many influences, and oppose many traditions. The young wife, for instance, may have been accustomed to much flattery, and may have entered on her new state of life imagining that everything was due to her, for since she had hitherto only studied her own tastes, neither family nor school could inspire her with devotion and sacrifice.

She may often come to her husband from out of a frivolous atmosphere, enervating flattery, and senseless adoration, young, foolish, and unfitted for the duties of married life, unprepared against danger, and with no preservative or safeguard against the illusions and deceptions of the world.

Is it then a matter of surprise that there should be some shortcomings?

All is not lost because there are perchance occasional outbursts of childish passion, varied at times by fits of extreme melancholy and extraordinary depression.

The woman confided to the hands of her husband is a jewel of great price, but often one that has not been sufficiently wrought and purged of all dross.

It is the husband's task to complete the work already begun, to polish and impart to it the final lustre and the final brightness. He must not take too much notice of the stains and be disproportionately anxious about them; the greater the love, the greater the shock at finding them where they were least expected, but he must take advantage of his position to try and efface them without giving way to despair.

True happiness is in his own hands, if he only knows how to win it.

Many men make to themselves an ideal of perfection, and then complain that the reality does not come up to their imagination. It is the task of those who are husbands to try and make everything come up to the ideal, and to instil into those they love everything which will render them still more precious.

It will not do to be hasty; it will be better to imitate the wise deliberation of Providence. When matters are precipitated things will not prosper, and feelings will be wounded. If an attempt is made to uproot the tares before their time, the good grain will get loosened, and thus the whole harvest, which might have been saved by the exercise of a little patience, will be endangered.

Some men are irritated at the least imperfection; in the presence of anything that annoys them they act passionately, or exhibit an excess of sensibility. Others shut their eyes, and from love of peace completely conceal their feelings of annoyance and displeasure. Some neglect their homes, others lay them waste, and offer as their contribution nothing but sorrow.

A wife is sometimes discouraged, or even driven to despair, in consequence of the neglect to which she is subjected, or the continual shocks that she is compelled to endure. How can she act unless she be guided? How can she be expected to correct her faults of hastiness of character if the conduct exercised towards her can only tend to irritate and exasperate her. In this way deceptions are multiplied and sorrows accumulated.

In this way the domestic hearth, which should have been the abode of holy and pure affections, becomes sad and desolate; and if the husband and wife return to it, it is more from a sense of duty than of attraction. The consequence is natural enough, for though on the one hand living affections exercise attraction, on the other the fear of contradiction and the certain conviction of disagreements produce the contrary effect.

The most deplorable feature of the case is that often he who is most to blame, he who is the cause of these dissensions, and he who opens out to the future these sad prospects, is not only ignorant of the fact, but is even persuaded that the whole fault is on the other side, and that he is alone irreproachable.

Let us now turn to a very different picture—to that presented by the due exercise of authority in the family circle.

If concord and peace reign therein, it is not because it has always been exempt from the causes of trouble; it is most probable that the horizon has been heavy, and that many clouds have been seen in the distance; but wise and prudent parents have early prevented their formation, by carrying into these threatening shadows the light of love and truth.

Let such parents be the model for all you whom I am addressing. Do not expect full perfection in this world. Your duty and work should consist in the development of the germs of good that God has sown in the family, in hindering the growth of evil, or, if possible, circumscribing it and opposing its most fatal results.

God will bless such efforts, and make them more and more productive in the future, and more capable of bringing forth fruits of grace both in time and in eternity.

ELEVENTH CONFERENCE.

UNITY OF FAMILY LIFE (CONTINUED).—OBSTACLES.—DIVERSITY OF TASTES.

We have already laid down the principle that whatever the diversity of characters, none are radically bad, or incapable of being improved by cultivation; we have likewise ascertained that there are none so pure and unalloyed that they stand in no need of correction.

The end for which you parents have to strive to attain is therefore victory over yourselves, and the moral education of the souls and dispositions that are entrusted to you—duties which are in fact incumbent upon all, and necessary at every period of history. This is the end which must in a special manner be the aim of the head of the family, since he has to look not only to himself, but to those confided to him; and he cannot be said to fulfil this, his whole duty, unless he adds to the vigilance necessary for his own welfare the same amount of vigilance over all those who belong to him.

We must now consider a matter closely allied to that which we have just mentioned.

What, for example, is more closely connected with the character than tastes and sympathies? We find in them the same variety, and often the same contradictions; it seems that Nature, because she indefinitely diversifies the types from which she makes us, and the moulds in which she casts us, takes a pleasure in bringing into existence the strangest combinations. She often places side by side in one family the most contrary tendencies, unites in the same blood, and places under the same roof, a multitude of aspirations, preferences and desires, between which there is but little sympathy or resemblance.

It is easy to understand the difficulties that must necessarily ensue.

If, for example, two powerful steeds were harnessed together who refused to keep the same pace, or even to go in the same direction, it would be a matter of difficulty, especially for an unpractised hand, to drive them.

In such a case the journey would be perilous, and probably accompanied with disaster. The experienced and able horseman would, on the contrary, make light of such trifling difficulties, and be all the better pleased if he were given an impatient and impetuous team to direct.

The chariot of the family is entrusted to the parents! it must advance without deviation, and as much as possible without any shocks or concussions.

How can parents direct and keep together the family chariot of tastes and sympathies which are at variance? How bring to unity movements which not only are unequal in intensity, but are inclined to go in opposite directions? The task will be difficult, and one that will require much care and experience.

It will be our task to study the variety of tastes that manifest themselves amongst mankind in general, and especially amongst the members of one family, and to consider carefully how this variety of tastes should be treated.

I.

Human language borrows from the natural order the word which expresses the dispositions of the soul.

Taste is a sense endowed by God with greater or less force by which we discern the savour of things, a kind of sentinel placed at the outposts of one of the most important functions of life; a thing that is ever on the alert, and makes us at once discern what is agreeable and what unpleasant, what is useful and what is hurtful; it is a kind of official admonitor, which sometimes allows itself to be corrupted by the outside world with whom it has sympathies and antipathies.

Nothing is more fanciful than the appreciations it transmits. We know that objects which are similar do not convey to every individual the same impression; but of all the senses with which man is endowed, this of which I speak is the most effectually subjective, and that in which individuality most strongly asserts itself.

In every eye that is not diseased the same colour produces the same picture; in every delicate ear the same sound calls up the same sensation; but the case is quite different with the sense of taste: the food which delights the one palate is disagreeable and even sometimes repulsive to the other. The fact that such divergencies exist is well known and admitted by all.

That which is true of physical taste is also true of the spiritual. Certain propensities appear to be general, and certain tendencies to be more or less common to all; but even here we find a multitude of differences in detail, which must of necessity be productive of contradictions in the special application.

One man has exalted tastes; another is carried away by what is base and unruly; a third scarcely feels any inclination towards doing what is wrong;

whilst a fourth has a peculiar dislike, a sort of intuitive objection, to everything legitimate, and relishes nothing but what is opposed to the rules of law and order: "*Nitimur in vetitum.*"

Whilst there are many persons who take pleasure in the society of the dissipated, and go to the extreme of worldly amusements, others are only happy when leading a retired life of complete seclusion.

Luxury and display commend themselves by their alluring fascinations to a large proportion of mankind, but simplicity and moderation also find their partisans. Some persons can only endure life in towns or cities, whilst others are never happy unless they are in the country. Society is indispensable to some, whilst others prefer retirement. Business and a sort of restless activity are the dream of some men, and the quiet which would be death to them fills up the measure of the aspirations of many of their fellow-creatures.

Whilst one person cannot resign himself to spend much of his time away from home, another is never contented unless he is away; what seems most delightful to one is most distasteful to another. In short, nothing is more contradictory and more intensely diversified than the tendencies and the inclinations of mankind.

Whence comes this difference?

Is it the work of nature or of liberty? Is it innate, original, and independent of our actions; or are we, on the contrary, answerable for a great part of it, and does it flow as from its source from free choice?

Many tastes are doubtless hereditary, but others are formed later on by ourselves, which carry and deposit the seed of our autonomy.

The first are the effect of our constitution, our temperament, and our character.

It is evident that a hasty and impetuous nature will feel other attractions and other wants than one whose distinctive feature is procrastination and indolence.

Both the blood and the nerves play a considerable part; age also exercises a great influence, a circumstance which has furnished to poets the famous picture of habits incidental to the various seasons of life.

The atmosphere in which we were born and nurtured has also its place in the multiplicity of causes which concur towards a certain and fixed result.

But the greatest cause incontestably belongs to our personal individuality—I mean to our inward faculties, to the greater or less degree of our sensibility, to the bend of our minds, the inclination of our will, and the impetuosity of our desires.

That which makes us individually different one

from the other, is at the same time the source of a whole multitude of particular attractions.

In addition to the centre of gravity common to all, each one has his own special centre, whose influence is felt, even when contradicted and resisted.

These individual tastes can always be corrected and reformed by a willing effort; sometimes even they can be completely uprooted and given another direction.

To return to our first simile, it is well known that man's palate gradually becomes accustomed to any taste, and that it may acquire a liking for things for which it formerly felt repugnance.

Habit takes away from them their first sharpness and acidity, and at last transforms into a feeling of pleasure what was once a disagreeable sensation.

In every education carried out with intelligence people are careful to help a child to triumph over a repugnance towards healthy food, which seems to be instinctive; but surely the correction of a child's moral tastes is a far more important part of the mission confided to parents.

The work begins with the first hours of life; for the spontaneous instincts of the young nature are at once manifested.

The intellect, as yet enclosed in the most delicate organs, is to all outward appearance buried in a deep sleep; but even then there are preferences which assert themselves, temptations to which the will is subjected, and attractions which it is unable to resist. If parents do not interpose at the right moment with wisdom and prudence, the incline will become more steep, and the movement more irresistible; and though they may try to check it, they will not be able to do so without inflicting a severe wound. The wound no doubt is salutary and beneficial, but it would have been much less cruel if, through greater attention, the formation of the habit, which afterwards gives so much trouble to destroy, had been earlier prevented. Parents too often neglect their duty in this respect; they not only are unable to repress or discipline the natural tastes, but they often inspire or develop those that are replete with danger.

It may be a taste for luxury or exaggerated expenditure which they encourage; they perhaps consider nothing too good for the personal adornment of a child, and nothing too precious to satisfy its fancies. In this way they unconsciously foster an incipient vanity; and the child, exposed upon the theatre of life as upon a stage, soon learns to believe in its own worth and importance.

Each of its words is treasured up, even when it oversteps the barrier of respect and seemliness; each burst of humour is encouraged and applauded, and every word issuing from its lips is taken in good part and accepted like an oracle.

Its every desire is complied with, and its every wish gratified; its amusements are the all-important business for those around it, and owing to a deplorable fashion which is being introduced everywhere in our day, it is already initiated to all that worldly gatherings can offer, that is exciting to a heart so fresh and open to impressions.

It is, perhaps, taken to representations that are said to be suitable to its age, but which reveal things it had better not have known, or to gatherings where there are dances, apparently innocent and simple, but which are sure to raise feelings of premature excitement.

In this way many parents forestall the time marked out by Providence for the child to acquire such knowledge, and seem as if they were anxious to hasten on the terrible crisis, which will but too soon come to unfold its formidable mysteries.

Parents should not grudge to the morning of life the serenity of its heaven, the gentle freshness of its morning dew. They should hesitate to unsettle the conscience, still so pure, to accumulate clouds, to make the lightning flash and the storm burst forth.

It is sad to see them destroy with their own hands that earthly paradise which the Divine mercy, in spite of Adam's sin, still leaves to the first years of our existence.

It is a bitter thought, that too often the imprudence and folly of parents prematurely breaks the charm, and brings to an abrupt end that first period of innocent security, of peaceful and blessed slumber, which can, alas, never return and bring back its thrice blessed illusions.

I implore all parents who hear me, in the name of all that is most tender and most sacred in that title, to shield with their utmost care the souls that rest in a state of innocence, and to prevent them from being disturbed before they have arrived at the proper time to open their own eyes to the knowledge of good and evil. *"Adjuro vos . . ne suscitetis eam donec ipsa velit."*

Let them beware how they hasten, through their fault, the moment of those fearful struggles, the very thought of which should already fill them with dread.

They should be careful never to permit any pernicious tastes or fatal habits, which would quickly become the torment of their lives, to find their way into these young and impressionable hearts. It is not necessary to forbid children all society, or to blame all distractions and suppress all amusements; but amongst these recreations and amusements parents should distrust those which take no account of the distinctions of age; they should dread the proud display which exalts a child in its own estimation above its due, and causes it to attribute to itself ridiculous importance; they should fear indiscreet assemblies, in which the sexes are too much brought together; they should regard as dangerous doubtful representations, in which, under the appearance of an innocent plot, objectionable sentiments find their way, and where they fear that voluptuousness reigns supreme.

It cannot be said that the child's eyes are still veiled, for in a moment the cloud will burst and the light of day pour in; it cannot be said that his ears do not hear, for they are only too open and too ready to understand.

Were there even no further drawback than to turn away children from taking delight in simple pleasures from those that are at hand, and in which all can easily partake, I should still see in this substitution a real misfortune and great danger, both for the present and for the future.

The practical conclusion to arrive at from what we have just considered, is that one of the most important and most grave duties that parents have to perform is to stem as early as possible the formation, generally so rapid, of those instincts and tastes, which would increase with great rapidity, and finally end in the production of the most tyrannical practices.

I should like to ask those blind parents who allow their indulgence to degenerate into weakness, and who for the sake of avoiding contradiction let loose every fancy, what it is they are endeavouring to accomplish, and what they are desirous of attaining?

What will be the result of a weak and cowardly education but a self-willed nature, which expects everything to yield to it—a lazy and selfish being, who only desires to seek his own gratification, and an unsociable man, who will render others as well as himself miserable.

The case would still be worse if we entered into details upon the depraved tastes which the parents doubtless do not themselves inspire (for there are none so unnatural as to go that length), but from which they have not known sufficiently well how to preserve or protect those confided to them.

These depraved tastes arise from the society of bad companions, and from intercourse with those amongst whom a certain amount of laxity is prevalent. Too much liberty in early years, friendships contracted at school, licence in conversation, and passionate attraction for light and worthless literature, are the principal sources where our youth, and, alas! we must also add, the child only just ushered into years of discretion, draw their perverted tastes, which are productive of so many deviations from the right path, and whose first result is to cause the family vexation and trouble, and perhaps even disunion and revolt against parental authority.

How are these great stumbling-blocks to be avoided?

What system should be pursued, and what treatment adopted, in the delicate and difficult task of managing different tempers and contradictory tastes?

Such is the important question which we must now try to solve.

II.

Domestic government, applied to what concerns this subject (as in other cases already indicated), is susceptible of taking three distinct forms and following three distinct courses.

The first form is that of an absolute and autocratic system; in many houses the taste and temper of one individual is imposed in such a manner that every one is obliged to bend before it and submit to its dictation.

When the dominant spirit is not that of the natural and lawful head of the family, as is often the case, the evil is great; but it becomes infinitely greater when it is only that of an individual member occupying a subordinate position, when whatever he dislikes is entirely proscribed, and whatever has his sympathy and approbation is the rule for the entire household.

Let us take as an example a grown-up son or daughter or friend, who is of strong mind and decided character, with a will which I am not supposing to be dishonest, but only one that takes the lead in everything, and legislates for the entire household.

In this case the family lose all individuality, and only appreciate what pleases the ruling spirit: they take no account of their own legitimate desires and wishes, they renounce their own ideas, preferences and opinions, and undergo the weight of a moral pressure from without which nothing can counterbalance.

Sometimes an anonymous, invisible, and irresponsible influence succeeds in grasping the command—the more dangerous, inasmuch as it cannot be reached, and the heavier to bear because its action unceasingly reopens unhealed wounds.

Some parents are not satisfied at becoming themselves slaves, unless they can drag all their family along with them, and make their own shame reflect itself on them, and in this way condemn those around them to drink to the dregs the chalice of their own humiliation. This kind of usurpation is utterly out of place, and much to be deplored.

I have already pointed out a species of absolute authority which is exercised by children; I have spoken of the childish and imperious wills to which parents at first yield from love and affection, but to which they are finally compelled to submit.

It is not necessary to dwell upon this anomaly. I will merely say, that whatever be its cause or origin, the sacrifice of the liberty of the many to that of the individual must always be a crying injustice and an immense misfortune.

The injustice is the more disastrous because it either lowers or subverts real authority; the misfortune is the greater inasmuch as it is aggravated by an infinity of sufferings that penetrate into the smallest details of life.

A family in this condition is like an invalid who is unable to make the least movement of the body without finding that such movement paralyses the various members.

As long as he remains perfectly quiet, he feels comparatively little suffering; but if he attempts to make the slightest movement, he realises at once the seriousness of his condition and the extent of his infirmity.

Such is more or less the case with a family in which one absolute will imposes itself on those around it.

If complete stagnation does not ensue, it will perpetually chafe under the slavery to which it is compelled to submit. Many members of a family yield because they have not sufficient energy to make opposition, and unwillingly submit to what is in reality a moral compulsion.

Such a course may produce external obedience, but internal disaffection is sure to exist.

If such submission on the part of the many to these inexorable demands were productive of the good of all, the case would assume a different aspect, but, on the contrary, it is productive of evil. The concessions that are made are made to the detriment of the family at large, and of those very persons who are the object of them.

The mother sees this clearly, and the hard necessity imposed upon her subjects her to a twofold torture, especially as she is given no credit for it.

The will accustomed to see everything bend before it easily becomes persuaded that such a state of things is natural, and considers it fitting and proper that those around it should be in subjection, or they would be failing in the due performance of their duty.

What is more strange still, by an extraordinary aberration, he to whom everything is given up is unable to appreciate what is done for him, but declares that he is a victim, and imagines that he is obliged to submit to the undue exercise of authority, and that his wishes are not regarded.

To avoid this excess, the family often run into the opposite extreme. There is no longer a unity produced by one will imposing itself upon others, and subjecting them to its power, but in its place a complete chaos, caused by the undue liberty accorded to each individual to pursue his own tastes and follow exclusively his own pleasures.

The father listens to his own desires, and gives himself wholly up to them, to the entire neglect of those who are entrusted to his care and protection; the mother equally turns in the direction of her natural inclinations, heedless of the duties involved in her position; and the children, with the double example thus given them, do not fail, as soon as they begin to feel their own power, to run after what pleases and fascinates them.

A semblance of peace is thus attained; for it is evident that since no instincts are contradicted, no tastes thwarted, and each is allowed to glide without hindrance down the inclined plane whereon nature has placed him, the family may imagine that all is prosperous.

One voice alone, in such cases, is heard in protest, and this voice, though all wish to stifle it, arises from the depths of the heart, accompanied with remorse and bitter regrets; it is the voice of duty, the voice of blood and natural affection, the cry of an innate feeling, and the solemn remonstrance of nature.

What has become of the family?

We seek for it, but cannot find it. We certainly find persons living under the same roof, and meeting day by day at stated periods, because habit requires it and necessity demands it; but this of itself does not constitute the family.

The table is prepared, and guests periodically take their places at it; the sound of appellations which would seem to point out the existence amongst these distinct individualities of eternal links and the most indissoluble bonds that can be formed between human creatures are heard, but nevertheless, under all these appearances the habits and affections which such things presuppose, cannot be discerned.

After meeting for a few minutes at a time, and exchanging, often briefly and coldly, a few insignificant phrases, or holding one of those conversations for which matter is seldom wanting, even to perfect strangers, all quickly disperse, equally happy to return as soon as possible to their various pursuits and practices.

It is quite evident that they were present only in body; even when assembled together and seated side by side at table that their minds were absent, and that they were surrounded by a network of prepossessions, recollections and hopes, which held them fast to the external atmosphere that absorbed all the interest of their lives.

Under the hypothesis we are supposing, all this is accomplished without mutual reproach.

The liberty allowed to each is not only an established fact, but has been elevated to the importance of a law. Each one has agreed to put no constraint on his own actions or on those of his neighbour. Each one has agreed that the only means of obtaining peace in the home circle is to take as a principle unlimited tolerance, and consequently (for the things are seldom separated) an almost universal indifference.

Once this maxim is adopted, what can become more easy or more simple? Each one chooses his own path, and in its pursuit indulges in every possible gratification.

There is no need to dwell upon this. I have already said more than enough to show that such a system can only be erected upon the ruins of what is most dear to us.

Before establishing itself, it had to sacrifice confidence and shiver into atoms both domestic happiness and domestic affection. How is it possible that a husband and wife who are truly devoted to each other can desire this false liberty?

How can a father, who is worthy of the name, detach himself from what concerns the virtue, the honour, and the future welfare of his children, or be content to regard with a look of indifference transactions capable of compromising these great questions and not attempt to interfere? And yet the picture I have drawn is by no means fanciful; it faithfully depicts what takes place in many a home in consequence of the license introduced by modern manners and customs.

It involves positive disaffection, the rupture of the most sacred ties, and the entire destruction of the unity of the family.

Things cannot reach this point without great deceptions and great sufferings, and when such is the case, can there be any possible prospect of happiness?

Whatever be the drawbacks of personal power, they can never entail so much suffering as the complete absence of any head and the want of all governing authority.

We are fortunately not reduced to make a choice between these two evils.

The real line of action, or rather the only one that can lead to the goal and conduct the whole family into the regions of peace and concord, is as far removed from the one as from the other. And yet the most strongly marked and refractory tasks are capable of being blended together, united, and led to embrace with good will that which was formerly repugnant and distasteful.

Ardent love daily produces greater transformations than this: it makes people seek out, not that which commends itself, but that which is distasteful, not personal satisfaction in a loved enjoyment, but a bitter relish in the forgetfulness of self.

It is easy, with the most contrary tendencies, to live in peace and concord, if each one thinks less of ministering to his own individual happiness than of attending to that of others—if he finds more satisfaction in pleasing those around him than in the gratification of himself. That which is destructive of everything else is selfishness, and selfishness often finds its way into the holiest and purest affections.

Self-gratification is productive of many obstacles, makes men fall back perpetually on themselves, and does not allow them to lose self-consciousness for a moment. Even the love of wife and children can be sometimes interested: a man can, for instance, worship himself, and think of his own comforts, whilst he imagines that he is devoting himself to his family. He may obstinately persist in demanding a return for his affections, be astonished when this retribution is refused him, and be chafed if, instead of receiving attentions, he is obliged to give them; all the time ignorant that such is the great law of love which our Lord Himself consecrated when He spoke those Divine words: "*Melius est dare quam accipere*"—"It is better to give than to receive." These words are a paradox to every calculating mind, and every personal feeling that is too exclusive, but are nevertheless the true expression of real love, which is never so complete as when it has the opportunity of sacrificing itself for those it loves.

Let us now cast a glance at the family, and see what should be the true character of its relationships.

The wife should live less for herself than for the husband whom she has sworn to comfort, help and console.

The father should breathe, not for himself, but for the wife in whom is centred all his devotion, and for the children in whom are centred all his hopes and expectations, who will perpetuate his name, and preserve and increase the patrimony of honour which they will one day inherit.

The children, on their part, should have no nobler ambition than to respond to paternal affections, without ever deceiving their expectations.

If all the various members of the family circle

are filled with these sentiments, they will have no difficulty in sacrificing certain particular inclinations for the sake of adapting themselves to those they find around them.

A struggle may sometimes occur; but it will be a struggle in which each one will strive, not to obtain the success of his own wishes, but rather to throw them into the shade and sacrifice them to those of others.

Mutual concessions, softened as they are in this case by the feeling which inspires them and by the satisfaction which accompanies them, have in them nothing sad; on the contrary, when they are made by a generous and devoted heart, they contain inexhaustible treasures of happiness.

But even should the name of self-denial and sacrifice be dreaded, there is another remedy at hand. These tastes, so diverse in their origin, can be gradually brought together and assimilated; and the higher they soar, the less will become the distance that separates them. Nothing is more worthy of notice than this fact with regard to our ideas.

People of ordinary intellectual capabilities continually come into collision and contradict each other's sentiments, with scarcely a single point on which they can agree. But the case is quite different with intellects of a higher order, who meet without difficulty upon a common ground: though differences may still exist, the higher the intellect, the less are they discernible—like the rays of the sun scattered over the face of the earth, they join nearer and nearer as they ascend their focus, and are at length all blended in one common centre.

Æsthetical tastes, for instance, when carefully cultivated and directed, do not abandon themselves to the region of pure fancy, in which there are as many sentiments as there are persons, but make steady progress to perfection. The love of the beautiful forms a common ground on which every one may meet; every one, for instance, is unanimous in admiring a true masterpiece of art, and this upon the strength of personal impression, not upon the dictum of anyone else, as is usually the case with those who are ignorant and uneducated.

What is true of art, of literature, and of poetry is equally true of everything else.

In order to draw the tastes of mankind towards unity, men must be gradually elevated, and the further they are removed from all that is base and vile, the nearer they will approach a mutual understanding, and the greater will be the harmony of their appreciations.

It is the base and low inclinations, the carnal and gross attractions of mankind, that produce a want of unity and draw men in different directions; the more we free ourselves from them, the more do we become unfettered, the nearer do we approach, and the more do we appreciate, only what is great. The beautiful, the good and the true, the threefold radiation of the divinity upon the human soul, begins then to recall our desires that had strayed away, and to rally our scattered aspirations; we turn towards the common centre, and we enter thereby into the current which carries with it every noble and exalted soul.

I cannot repeat too often, that if parents desire to preserve their children from harm, and to succeed in the difficult undertaking of their education, this will be the best course to pursue. It is the parents who must form their tastes and inspire them with the love of what is great and what is pure, and this not only in the order of moral and religious questions, but also in what is material.

Children should unquestionably be trained to admire virtue, to love and respect the manifestations of God in humanity, as taught in the holy truths of a revealed religion, and to have an admiration for the great events of history; but below this higher order of things are others which no one need fear to make them love, and which can fitly claim a large share in their esteem and affections.

Nature and art, the works of the Creator, and the imitations made by the hand of man, eloquence, poetry, the fine arts, all the divers forms of literature, without mentioning the positive sciences, wherein, in seeking only for what is true, we so often find also what is beautiful—all these form a vast field for study. Parents must take their children by the hand, and seek to awaken within them the spontaneous attractions which cry: "*Sursum corda*"—"Let us lift up our hearts." They must teach them to despise what is trivial and common, and to bestow all their sympathy on objects that tend to elevate and refine the mind. Parents may rest assured that after having formed and raised the inclinations of those entrusted to them, they will find themselves able to make common cause upon a multitude of practical questions, the application of which in special cases is sure to follow.

The young man of refined taste will despise worthless literature, and have a repugnance for impure spectacles and vulgar company. He will prefer to associate with men of culture and education, in whose society, though he may not be free from all dangers, he will run no risk of becoming vitiated or corrupted.

He will seek out amongst the amusements and distractions presented to him those which are in accordance with the aspirations that have been cultivated in him. And even if these amusements should have a hold upon his senses, the danger is very much diminished when he is alive to what is objectionable in them, and is accustomed to value things on their own intrinsic merit.

I will conclude this conference with the words of Scripture: "*Omnia munda mundis*" — "To the pure all things are pure."

In order to traverse unsoiled the miry paths of the world, we must have an eye that looks beyond them, and a heart endowed with a taste that disdains them.

Endeavour, then, to create in yourselves, and to develop in those around you, these noble instincts; you will then experience no difficulty in gathering together the desires and inclinations of all into one common sheaf, whose blessed union will be your strength, and give you, as it were, a foretaste of the joys of heaven.

TWELFTH CONFERENCE.

UNITY OF FAMILY LIFE (CONTINUED).—OBSTACLES.— PLEASURE.

The consideration of the great diversity of tastes and characters that exists amongst men leads us, as a natural consequence, to the important question of diversity in pleasures and enjoyments.

Where should men seek for amusements ?—which are not as some imagine, entirely unnecessary and superfluous, but really an indispensable element of life.

To what extent may they be accepted and made use of ?

How can any inherent danger in them be avoided, and how can they be leavened so that they may become healthy and innocuous ?

These are always momentous questions, but they have nowadays assumed such an additional importance, that we may look upon them as the most difficult and indispensable problem we have to solve.

It is not my intention to examine them in detail.

I will merely treat of them in their direct bearing towards the subject of these conferences.

Endeavouring, as we are, to satisfy ourselves as to the causes which ordinarily intercept the unity that should exist in the family circle, it is impossible that we should not consider the question of pleasure, and ascertain whether it will prove a help or an obstacle.

Are we to hope that it will aid our work, or to fear that it should destroy it? Will it become the cement of the edifice we are striving to erect, or prove a dissolving matter, capable of threatening its solidity and causing its ruin?

It is a vexed question, and one capable of receiving various solutions, according to the various ideas formed upon the subject.

There are three different kinds of pleasure: the first is that which belongs by right to the domestic hearth, or is incidental to it; the second is that which is sought for from without, but nevertheless can be enjoyed in the society of the family; the third is the pleasure which should be styled isolated, because each individual member of the same family pursues it alone, and follows it to the complete exclusion of those who belong to him. It is evident that these three kinds of pleasure are very different in their essence and origin.

We must consider each of them separately, in

order to form a right appreciation of their different advantages and disadvantages, and to ascertain which may be indulged in, which should only be tolerated with precaution and reserve, and which should be utterly rejected.

I.

Let us first take into consideration the pleasure of the domestic hearth, which is at the same time the purest and the least dangerous.

This pleasure necessarily assumes a calm and moderate aspect; its promises are possibly less brilliant than those in other quarters, but more true; its display is less splendid, but its impressions are always more agreeable, for material enjoyment is not much in itself when the heart has no share in it. The mind is always more at ease in close and intimate gatherings, where all are well known to each other, and where all hearts beat in unison, than it is when in the company of the outside world. The spectacle of these gatherings is worthy of all praise, and causes a cry of admiration to burst forth from the mouth of the prophet: "*Quam bonum et quam jucundum habitare fratres in unum*"—"How good and agreeable a thing it is for brethren to dwell together in unity."

The family circle should never be so exclusive as to close its doors to all strangers; but, as a rule, it should only admit those who sympathise with its ideas and habits. From time to time it may be widened, and admit within its pale a society of people still further removed from its particular and special interests; but such society should be very carefully selected, and should itself become purified and invigorated, by entering this holy sanctuary, wherein reigns a divinity that ensures its eternal peace.

The children, under the loving supervision of affectionate parents, will indulge in innocent and unrestrained amusements, free from any exaggerated propriety or affectation; their pleasures will be simple, suitable, and full of dignity. They will never exhibit any strained intercourse, insincere friendships, or any insipid and untruthful style of conversation.

Such a family will never deal in any of that counterfeit coin which circulates so largely in the outside world, and which, though never satisfactory, is accepted as inevitable, and traded in by the general mass of the community.

As this pleasure of the domestic circle is purer, so also is it less dangerous than the other two. I do not say there is no danger whatever, for pleasure retains everywhere its own nature, but it is much less formidable when placed under the protection of our most cherished affections, when seeking the approval of parents, and taking for its ground and witness the spot wherein are assembled our best and holiest recollections.

Parents have much power, in such a case, to inspire moderation and the exercise of discretion.

The walls of the home have their voice; the precepts and admonitions of the father are engraved upon them, and remain adherent to every part of the domestic temple; everything can, if necessary, recall the protecting rules of respect and honour, and proclaim the laws of a holy reserve and strict and scrupulous modesty. If the family be really Christian in fact as well as in name, the whole house will be pervaded with the special presence of the Almighty, enabling it to be said of those who dwell within its walls that they rejoice in the face of the Lord: "*Exultant justi in conspectu Dei.*"

Are not these exceptionally favourable conditions for the preservation of that which parents should be most anxious to secure to those whom Heaven has placed in their keeping?

The task of the father is to provide his children innocent amusements, in which he himself can take the initiative and superintend and direct the details.

If the education of the children is one of the principal parts of a parent's duty, that of procuring recreations suited to their age and dispositions, is scarcely less important.

Happy are the parents who succeed in rendering the home more agreeable and more attractive than any other place, and in making their children love it, not only through gratitude and a sense of duty, but also through the natural predilection engendered by the satisfaction of all legitimate wishes.

Happy the parents whose children remain at home because they are nowhere else so happy and so contented.

It was formerly more easy to inspire this preference, because families were more numerous, and each one found in his home a society which he is now often forced to seek elsewhere; because tastes were simpler, life quieter, and prevailing habits did not to such an extent scatter the various members of the family.

It will be the triumph of parental prudence and tact to obtain by dint of love that which was once a natural circumstance, it will be a miracle of wisdom to regulate matters so that the comparison between distractions indulged in out of the house, and those that are found within, should always be to the advantage of the latter, and that if a struggle should burst forth between contrary aspirations, those which lead to the centre, and make desires converge towards the home, should be victorious.

II.

According as the horizon widens and social relationships are multiplied, we have less guarantee for satisfaction as to the amusements indulged in.

The world flocks to theatres, social gatherings, and the thousand and one trifles which bewilder and amuse it.

If there were in these things nothing but an inoffensive recreation, the father could without fear permit his son to indulge in them, and the mother would need to exercise but little supervision over her daughter. Parents themselves can say by experience whether such a security is possible.

Though the excesses and extravagances of the stage may not alarm them for themselves, the question assumes a completely different aspect with reference to the young who are confided to their care.

There is good reason to fear the scenes that are exhibited, and the words that are made use of on the stage. There is perhaps even more reason to dread the crowds that frequent the theatres, the spectacle of luxury and extravagance that they exhibit, and the heterogeneous elements they bring together.

The probability is that this atmosphere, impregnated as it too often is with a spirit of voluptuousness, will intoxicate minds that are weak and young, and fill them with excitemeut; and if perchance a poisoned arrow should effect an entry into their hearts, there will be no possibility of its being removed without the infliction of a cruel wound.

Balls and social gatherings exercise such a fascination on the minds of simple and inexperienced souls, who are only acquainted with the bright side of life, and ignorant of its sufferings and its disenchantments, that they must of necessity be a cause of anxiety. Provided the parents are wise and prudent, they will not fail to see there is a middle course to pursue. Such parents will feel the necessity of exercising great caution in these matters, and will recognise the necessity of paying a due regard to age, to disposition, to circumstances, and to necessities; they will have to progress step by step, advancing by the aid of experience, watching for impressions, and modifying according to circumstances the line of action they had at first thought fit to adopt.

A father, who both understands his own mission and the character of those with whom he has to deal, will not for a moment lose sight of the action exercised from without, or of the impressions received from within; he will endeavour to find his way amidst the confusion of ideas in minds that are fresh and little acquainted with the realities of existence—signs and symptoms imperceptible to others, but full of meaning to him, will quickly reveal what is going on, every phase of which he will be able to understand.

But in no case should the pleasure sought for in the world exclude the society of the family circle.

If there be indeed a potent and sure antidote, capable of neutralising the poisonous draughts which often exist at the bottom of the cup of pleasure, I am convinced that none can be found better than that which I have suggested.

In the first place, in the presence of the father the choice will be more severe and more intelligent, more impartial and more judicious.

He possesses the knowledge of people and things, and knows how to assimilate the material dispositions of his children with those of the societies they are establishing an intercourse with, and is well able to make their recreations proportionate to their need. It is easy for him to thrust aside what is hurtful and unsuitable.

The first safeguard is the controlling action of the parents, who should make use of their matured judgment and discrimination for a conscientious choice and for a careful and attentive examination; they must neither commit the imprudence of exciting ardent desires by the refusal of all pleasure, or have the weakness to give such desires full vent to their passions.

The parents should initiate the child, by degrees, with due measure and precaution, to the joys and recreations of the youth, and the youth in his turn to the society and the amusements appertaining to the divers phases of the period he is passing through.

The more enlightened the choice, the less will be the danger.

What a safeguard to virtue not yet solidly established is the protection of this attentive eye, from which nothing escapes.

If it be true that the Christian man fears nothing in the various vicissitudes of life, because he feels that he is surrounded and sustained by the action of an invisible Providence which watches over each of his steps, and in which he hopes against every hope, can it not be also said that children will be sheltered when they feel themselves, as it were, clothed with the tender solicitude of that other providence nearer still, or rather, more accessible to their eyes, which like to the one in whose image it is made, carefully watches over their movements, and is always ready to help, and disposed to guide their steps and bring back the erring.

The respect alone which the father's presence inspires, is of itself a strength of no slight or trivial importance, and forms a rampart for protection; the thought sometimes, and still more the sight of this guardian angel sent by God Himself to shelter under his wings a life exposed to the illusions of inexperience and the attractions of first allurements, will oftentimes suffice to restrain, to direct, to reveal the threatening danger, and to indicate the opening path—in short, to inspire the courage of duty, and to cause the child to embrace it without fear or alarm.

It will scarcely be possible to destroy altogether the struggle which exists between the world and the family, for their cares and thoughts are opposed to each other, and their interests are often completely at variance. The world and the family are in fact two belligerent parties fighting for supremacy, each endeavouring to secure exclusively the affections of the young.

If, however, there is a chance of conciliation between the invitations they proffer, if the world can be frequented without prejudice to the family circle, and if the latter can preserve its compact unity without renouncing the intercourse offered to it; this desirable solution is undoubtedly to be found in the means I have pointed out.

The family, to be able to confront the enemy without undergoing any encroachment, must be like one man, without any division or separation, the father standing by the son, and the husband by the wife.

We may be sure that under such conditions there will be little risk of defeat; the sacred battalion will close its ranks, manifest no separation, and permit no breach of the fortress.

The father cannot always play the part of companion to his son, and his continuous presence, even if possible, far from being a help, would become an obstacle both absurd and annoying, which would eventually make each one dislike the society of the other, and be productive of much evil.

The father cannot be so closely attached to his sons as not to find himself sometimes in different places and among different people, but where he cannot be in person with his children, he can make them feel a moral presence, derived from the knowledge of the places they frequent and the persons and the society they cultivate.

Though he may not actually stand by the side of his son, he will have a representative of sure morality and of tried virtue. His business, his relations, the customs of the country, and the very confidence he owes to his friends, may prevent him from superintending personally the amusements and recreations of his children; but that need not prevent him from knowing the places that his son frequents, and every one that is admitted to them, or following the steps he takes, and hearing, as it were, every word of his conversations.

If the father is prudent, he will take into consideration different circumstances, be careful to show no symptoms of distrust, or exhibit any desire of restraining his children from a reasonable amount of liberty.

He must be ever on the watch to take notice of what is passing around him, and try to account to himself for everything; neither distance nor the thickness of walls should be able to stop his eye; he must have a sort of divine instinct, enabling him to obtain a complete knowledge of the child's character, so that nothing may entirely escape his notice, or remain for any length of time hidden from him.

If by chance some secret wound should be inflicted, he should be at once able to administer a suitable remedy.

I have now pointed out a few of the precautions which will be a help to disarm a danger imminent and inevitable, if the division of the family was necessarily entailed in the idea of pleasure.

III.

I designate as isolated pleasure that individual pleasure taken by each member of a family apart from the rest, when the tastes of each are different, and the preferences are of a purely personal character. When affection or a sense of duty do not succeed in overcoming these differences, the result is that invisible attractions draw the inmates of the same house into opposite directions.

One will remain at home, whilst another will live perpetually away, or if all equally desert the paternal roof, it will not be to go into the same company, but each to join in those kinds of festivities and gatherings that suit his own particular taste; the sons, from an early date, will begin to go out alone, and from the first moment of experiencing their liberty will seem to be unable to enjoy themselves except in places which are unfrequented by their parents.

The parents in their turn will be disunited, and the entire family will be like the poet of mythology, the members of whose body became an object of dispute between groups of people who were each anxious to possess a few morsels.

I do not claim to lay down any set of inflexible rules, but I assert that this dismemberment of an entirely united body can only afford a promise of great danger.

The first drawback of family disunion is, that it soon becomes natural, and the various members cease to have any common participation in joy or sorrow.

Home is no longer the centre; each one goes

elsewhere, and perpetually goes further and further away, because the thirst he feels, far from being satiated by such a method, is for ever on the increase; home becomes desolate and sterile, and the simple and sweet recreations it offers are but insipid, and without relish to the tongue long accustomed to other tastes.

Other places are preferred, and other gatherings, larger and more exciting, are sought after.

It is easy to foresee the result. The heart little by little becomes detached, and sometimes gradually, sometimes immediately, retires from the hallowed centre, where it should have found a permanent abode.

Moreover, its own centre being displaced, it begins henceforward, instead of turning towards the family, to submit to the attraction of another law, and to form, as it were, part of another world. The bond uniting relations together becomes distended and relaxed, and is sometimes altogether rent asunder.

This bond, however, is only external and visible on the surface, whilst others are contracted which keep the young riveted elsewhere by the closest ties.

Thus the unity of the family is weakened and dissolved in its most necessary and most intimate parts.

When joys are no longer experienced in common,

nothing but sorrow remains to be shared, and even this will be divided sooner or later.

If the various members of the family are accustomed to have a separate happiness, even family bereavement will scarcely have the power of bringing them together; and not even the grave of a father or a mother will be able to reawaken the affections that have been extinguished.

On the contrary, the death of those who had a right to their love will make them feel but more keenly that the last link is severed of a separation practically long ago accomplished.

After a momentary meeting at the side of a half-closed grave, they will return to their various pursuits, without taking any steps for effecting a reunion or evincing any desire to meet again in the future.

This isolation of pleasure necessarily threatens the unity of the family circle, and engenders a great danger for the virtue and purity of its members.

We are all weak, all accessible to the allurements which beset human nature; and, to use the language of Christian teaching, we are all hourly exposed to temptation.

The supreme grace which we daily ask of God is that He should not permit us to fall into temptation, a grace which the strongest and holiest of men must seek for as much as the weakest and those who are most prone to evil.

But this inherent weakness of the human frame is greatly increased, when we are deprived of our natural support.

Did not the Almighty Maker of all mankind, in the first day of our creation, utter these mysterious words?—"*Non est bonum hominem esse solum, faciamus et adjutorium simile sibi*"—"It is not good for man to be alone; let us make a helpmeet for him."

Even before man's fall, during the golden era of his innocence, it was not good for him to be alone, because he felt the want of a heart to beat in unison with his own, and a voice to repeat and echo his song of love.

It was not good for man to live alone after his fall, because he required consolation in his sorrow, support in his infirmity, and the help of a loving arm in his struggles and difficulties.

The words of Scripture are unmistakable on this point: "*Væ soli cum ceciderit, non habet sublaventem se*"—"Woe to him who is alone; if such a one fall, there is no one to raise him up" (Eccles. iv. 10).

The Almighty has created the family to testify to this want and to supply this urgent necessity.

How then can man presume to destroy in part the

wisdom of the Divine economy, so admirably suited to his condition and wants?

The enterprise in which the family must participate, and that which is the most important of all, is the enterprise of virtue and of eternal salvation.

He who is called to live in the world, and who has the honour and responsibility of being a parent, must never pursue an isolated course; if he should separate himself from his wife and children, he will lose the strength which should have sustained him, the dignity which should have upheld him in the path of honour, and he will run the risk of staining and compromising that which constituted the spotless beauty of his life and character.

If such would be the case with those who have arrived at an age of maturity and know the world and its temptations and dangers, how much more will it not be the case with the young man whose portion is inexperience, and who is sure to be led away by an attractive exterior!

If a vessel, for instance, weak, easy to be submerged, and without a helmsman, were suddenly launched upon the ocean, in the midst of hidden rocks and dangerous quicksands, would it not be at the mercy of tempests raging fiercely from every quarter, and exposed to terrible danger?—and yet the fury of the storm would be nothing in comparison to the absence of the practised eye and vigorous arm of the helmsman.

The post of the parent is at the helm, as well during the hour of pleasure as that of prayer or study; if it is suitable that he should accompany his children in the ascent of the steps that lead to God, it is still more necessary that he should not forsake them at a time when they are treading ground in which a false step may precipitate them to the bottom of an abyss.

At such a moment, when his presence would be so useful and beneficial, he should be at the side of his children, ready to stretch out his hand and cause them to return to the right path.

His strength should be made use of to support their weakness, and his firm wisdom and matured judgment should temper and restrain the passion and impetuosity of their early years.

Parents must not flatter themselves that they have fully accomplished the duties of their position if they have in any way neglected the supervision of those entrusted to them, at the very period of their life when they stood most in need of guidance and support.

They should not rest content with a mere participation in the interests, studies, religion, and pursuits of their children, but remember that it is necessary also to participate to some extent in their amusements and pleasures.

When children have been well-prepared for the battle of life, parents need have no anxiety at the thought of leaving them to their discretion.

Like eagles which are trained to look at the light of that deceptive sun by which so many are blinded before they are permitted to take their flight into open space, they may then wing their way through the vast area of liberty and of light, without risk and without danger.

THE END.

R. WASHBOURNE'S CATALOGUE OF BOOKS,

18 PATERNOSTER ROW, LONDON.

11 ——————— '78

NEW BOOKS.

The Little Garden of the Soul, with Epistles and Gospels for all the Sundays and Chief Festivals of the Year. Cloth, neat, 6d., also superior binding, with clasp, 1s. Without the Epistles and Gospels, in superior binding, 6d., embossed, 9d., roan, 1s., and better bindings. *See* page 30.

Inner Life of Pere Lacordaire, O.P. From the French, by the author of "The Knights of St. John." New edition, revised, 6s. 6d.

Life of the Venerable Elizabeth Canori Mora. Translated from the Italian, with Preface by Lady Herbert. With Photograph, 3s. 6d.

Lives of the Early Popes. St. Peter to St. Silvester. By Rev. Thomas Meyrick, M.A. 8vo., 4s. 6d.

Old Testament Tales. By Charles Walker. 12mo., 2s. 6d.

The Duties of Christian Parents. Conferences by Père Matignon. Translated by Lady Constance Bellingham, with Preface by Mgr. Capel, 12mo., 5s. [*In the Press.*

Short Meditations, for every day in the Year. By an anonymous Italian author. Translated by Dom Edmund J. Luck, O.S.B. Prefaced by a letter of recommendation from His Eminence Cardinal Manning, 12mo. Edition for the Regular Clergy, 2 vols., 9s. Edition for the Secular Clergy, 2 vols., 9s. [*In the Press.*

The Rejection of Catholic Doctrines, attributable to the Non-Realization of Primary Truths. Exemplified in Letters to a Friend on Devotion to the B.V.M., the Angels, and Saints. By a Layman, 8vo., 1s.

On what Authority do I accept Christianity? A Question for reasonable Members of the Church of England. 12mo., 6d.

Manual of Sacred Chant, containing the Ordinary of the Mass, the Psalms and Hymns of Vespers and Compline, &c., &c. Music and Words. By Rev. J. Mohr, S.J., 18mo., 2s. 6d.

** *Though this Catalogue does not contain many of the books of other Publishers, R. W. can supply any, no matter by whom they are published. All orders, so far as possible, will be executed the same day.*

School Books, *with the usual reduction*, Copy Books, and other Stationery, Rosaries, Medals, Crucifixes. Scapulars, Incense, Candlesticks, Vases, &c., &c., supplied.

Foreign Books supplied. The publications of the leading Publishers kept in stock. R. Washbourne's Catalogue of Books published in America, post free.

Litany B.V.M., in F. Major, for Chorus and Solo (S.A.T.B.) [or Unison, *ad lib*], with Organ accompaniment. Music by Baroness Emma Fremantle. 1s. Half price, 6d.

Manuel de Conversation. 12mo., 1s.

Allah Akbar—God is Great. An Arab Legend of the Siege and Conquest of Granada. From the Spanish. By Mariana Monteiro. Contents:—1. The Genius of the Alhambra. 2. The King Abu-Abd-Allah el Zogirbi. 3. Zegries and Abencerrajes. 4. The Cypress of the Sultana. 5. The Chamber of Lions. 6. The Judgment of God. 7. Hernan Perez del Pulgar. 8. The Triumph of the Ave Maria. 9. Gonzalo Fernandez de Cordova. 10. The Conquest of Granada. 11. The Last Adieu. 12mo., 3s. 6d.

Illustrated with Head Pieces from the pencil of Miss Henriqueta Monteiro, and elaborately bound in accordance with the Arabic.

The Fairy Ching; or the Chinese Fairies' Visit to England. By Henrica Frederic. 12mo., cloth extra, 1s., gilt edges, 1s. 6d.

What Catholics do not Believe. By the Right Rev. Bishop Ryan, Coadjutor to the Archbishop of St. Louis. 12mo., 1s.

Life of Fr. Benvenuto Bambozzi, O.M.C., of the Conventual Friars Minor. Translated from the Italian (2nd Edition) of Fr. Nicholas Treggiari, D.D. 12mo., 5s. [*In the Press.*

Life of St. Wenefred, Virgin Martyr and Abbess, Patroness of North Wales and Shrewsbury. By Rev. T. Meyrick, M.A. 2s.

OREMUS, A Liturgical Prayer Book: with the Imprimatur of the Cardinal Archbishop of Westminster. An adaptation of the Church Offices: containing Morning and Evening Devotions; Devotion for Mass, Confession, and Communion, and various other Devotions; Common and Proper, Hymns, Lessons, Collects, Epistles and Gospels for Sundays, Feasts, and Week Days; and short notices of over 200 Saints' Days. Also short Liturgical Devotions for Holy Week. For greater convenience, the Latin has been given of all the Psalms, Hymns, and other Prayers, occurring in the ordinary services of the Church, in which the Faithful take more or less part. 32mo., 452 pages, paper cover, 2s.; cloth, 2s. 6d.; embossed, red edges, 3s. 6d.; French morocco, 4s. 6d.; calf, 5s. 6d.; morocco, 6s.; Russia, 8s. 6d. Also in superior or more expensive bindings.

Are You Safe in the Church of England? A Question for Anxious Ritualists. By an Ex-Member of the Congregation of S. Bartholomew, Brighton [Charles Walker]. 8vo., 6d.

Practical Hints on the Education of the Sons of Gentlemen. By an Educator. 8vo., 1s.

Contents:—1. Introduction. 2. The Mind. 3. Preparatory Education. 4. The Existing System of Education. 5. How to Manage a Class. 6. The Educator. 7. A Plea for the Study of Language.

The Child of Mary's Manual. Compiled from the French. Second Edition, with the Imprimatur of the Bishop of Clifton. 1s.

Gathered Gems from Spanish Authors. By Mariana Monteiro, author of "The Monk of the Monastery of Yuste." 3s.

He would be a Soldier. Comedy. 2 Acts. Boys, 6d.

R. Washbourne, 18 Paternoster Row, London.

Fr. Power's Catechism: Doctrinal, Moral, Historical, and Liturgical. Fourth Edition, enlarged and improved. 3 vols., 12mo., 10s. 6d.

Fr. Power's Catechism of Christian Doctrine. 2 vols., 7s. 6d.

Stories of the Saints. By M. F. S. 12mo., 4th Series. Saints of the Early Church. 3s. 6d.; 5th Series, 3s. 6d.

The Holy Mass: The Sacrifice for the Living and the Dead. By Rev. M. Müller, C.SS.R. 12mo., 10s. 6d.

The Faith of our Fathers: Being a Plain Exposition and Vindication of the Church founded by our Lord Jesus Christ. By Most Rev. Archbishop Gibbons, 12mo. 4s.; paper covers, 2s. nett.

ADELSTAN (Countess), Sketch of her Life and Letters, From the French of the Rev. Père Marquigny, S.J. 1s. & 2s. 6d.

Adolphus; or, the Good Son. 18mo., 6d.

Adventures of a Protestant in Search of a Religion. By Iota. 12mo., 2s. and 3s. 6d.

AGNEW (Mme.), Convent Prize Book. 12mo., 3s. 6d.

A'KEMPIS—Following of Christ. Pocket Edition, 32mo., 1s.; embossed red edges, 1s. 6d.; roan, 2s.; French morocco, 2s. 6d.; calf or morocco, 4s. 6d.; gilt, 5s. 6d.; russia, with clasp, &c., 10s. 6d.; ivory, with rims and clasp, 15s., 16s., 18s.; morocco antique, with corners and clasps, 17s. 6d.; russia, ditto, ditto, 16s., 20s.

——— Imitation of Christ; with Reflections. 32mo., 1s.; Persian calf, 3s. 6d.; 12mo., 3s. 6d.; mor., 10s. 6d.; mor. ant. 25s.

——— The Three Tabernacles. 16mo., 2s. 6d.

Albertus Magnus. *See* Dixon (Rev. Fr. T. A.).

Album of Christian Art. Twenty-three original composition Professor Klein, in Vienna. 4to., 7s. 6d.

Allah Akbar—God is Great. An Arab Legend of the Siege and Conquest of Granada. From the Spanish. By Mariana Monteiro. 12mo., 3s. 6d.

ALLIES (T. W.), St. Peter; his Name and his Office. 5s.

Alphabet of Scripture Subjects. On a large sheet, 1s.; coloured, 2s., mounted to fold in a book, 3s. 6d.

ALZOG'S Universal Church History. 8vo., 3 vols., each 20s.

AMHERST (Rt. Rev. Dr.), Lenten Thoughts. 2s. 6d.

ANDERDON (Rev. W. H., S.J.), To Rome and Back. Fly-Leaves from a Flying Tour. 12mo., 2s.

ANDERSEN (Carl), Three Sketches of Life in Iceland. Translated by Myfanwy Fenton. 12mo., 2s. 6d.

Angela Merici (S.) Her Life, her Virtues, and her Institute. From the French of the Abbé G. Beetemé. 12mo., 4s. 6d.

Angela's (S.) Manual: a Book of Devout Prayers and Exercises for Female Youth. 2s.; Persian, 3s. 6d.; calf, 4s. 6d.

Angels (The) and the Sacraments. 16mo., 1s.

——— Month of the Holy Angels. By Abbé Ricard. 1s.

Angelus (The). A Monthly Magazine. 8vo., 1d. Yearly subscription, post free, 1s. 6d. Volume for 1876, cloth, 2s. 6d. 1877, 2s.

Anglican Orders. By Canon Williams. 12mo., 3s. 6d.
Anglicanism, Harmony of. *See* Marshall (T. W. M.).
Are You Safe in the Church of England? A Question for Anxious Ritualists. By an Ex-Member of the Congregation of S. Bartholomew, Brighton. 8vo., 6d.
ARNOLD (Miss M. J.), Personal Recollections of Cardinal Wiseman, with other Memories. 12mo., 2s. 6d.
ARRAS (Madame d') The Two Friends; or Marie's Self-Denial. 12mo., 1s.; gilt edges, 1s. 6d.
Ars Rhetorica. Auctore R. P. Martino du Cygne. 12mo., 3s.
Artist of Collingwood. 12mo., 2s.
Association of Prayers. *See* Tondini (Rev. C.).
Augustine (St.) of Canterbury, Life of. 12mo., 3s. 6d.
Aunt Margaret's Little Neighbours; or, Chats about the Rosary. 12mo., 3s.
BAGSHAWE (Rev. J. B.), Catechism of Christian Doctrine, illustrated with passages from the Holy Scriptures. 2s. 6d.
——— Threshold of the Catholic Church. A Course of Plain Instructions for those entering her Communion. 12mo., 4s.
BAGSHAWE (Rt. Rev. Dr.), The Life of our Lord, commemorated in the Mass. 18mo., 6d., bound 1s.; Verses and Hymns separately, 1d., bound 4d.
BAKER (Fr., O.S.B.), The Rule of S. Benedict. From the old English edition of 1638. 12mo., 4s. 6d.
Baker's Boy; or, Life of General Drouot. 18mo., 6d.
BAMPFIELD (Rev. G.), Sir Ælfric and other Tales. 18mo., 6d.; cloth, 1s.; gilt, 1s. 6d.
BARGE (Rev. T.), Occasional Prayers for Festivals. 32mo., 4d. and 6d.; gilt, 1s.
Battista Varani (B.), *see* Veronica (S.). 12mo., 5s.
Battle of Connemara. By Kathleen O'Meara. 12mo., 3s.
BAUGHAN (Rosa), Shakespeare. Expurgated edition. 8vo., 6s. The Comedies only, 3s. 6d.
Before the Altar. 32mo., 6d.
BELL'S Modern Reader and Speaker. 12mo., 3s. 6d.
BELLECIO (Fr.), Spiritual Exercises of S. Ignatius. Translated by Dr. Hutch. 18mo., 2s.
BELLINGHAM (Lady Constance) The Duties of Christian Parents. Conferences by Père Matignon. Translated. 12mo., 5s.
Bells of the Sanctuary,—A Daughter of St. Dominick. By Grace Ramsay. 12mo., 1s. and 1s. 6d.; stronger bound, 2s.
Benedict (S.), Abridged Explanation of his Medal. 1d.
——— The Rule of our most Holy Father S. Benedict, Patriarch of Monks. From the old English edition of 1638. Edited in Latin and English by one of the Benedictine Fathers of St. Michael's, near Hereford. 12mo., 4s. 6d.
Benedictine Breviary. 4 vols., 18mo., Dessain, 1870. 26s. nett; morocco, 42s. nett, and 47s. nett.
Benedictine Missal. Pustet, Folio, 1873. 20s. nett; morocco, 50s. nett, and 60s. nett. Dessain, 4to., 1862, 18s. nett; morocco, 40s. nett, and 50s. nett.

R. Washbourne, 18 Paternoster Row, London.

BENNI (Most Rev. C. B.), **Tradition of the Syriac Church of Antioch**, concerning the Primacy and Prerogatives of S. Peter and of his successors, the Roman Pontiffs. 8vo., 7s. 6d.

BENVENUTO BAMBOZZI (Fr., O.M.C.), of the Conventual Friars Minor, Life of, from the Italian (2nd edition) of Fr. Nicholas Treggiari, D.D. 12mo., 5s. *In the Press.*

Berchmans (Bl. John), **New Miracle at Rome**, through the intercession of Bl. John Berchmans. 12mo., 2d.

Bernardine (St.) of Siena, Life of. With Portrait. 12mo., 5s.

Bertha; or, the Consequences of a Fault. 8vo., 2s. 6d.

Bessy; or, the Fatal Consequence of Telling Lies. 12mo., 1s.; stronger bound, 1s. 6d.; gilt, 2s.

BESTE (J. R. Digby, Esq.), **Catholic Hours**. 32mo., 2s.; red edges, 2s. 6d.; roan, 3s.; morocco, 6s.

———— Church Hymns. (Latin and English.) 32mo., 6d.

———— Holy Readings. 32mo., 2s., 2s. 6d.; roan, 3s.; mor., 6s.

BESTE (Rev. Fr.), **Victories of Rome**. 8vo., 1s.

Bible. Douay Version. 12mo., 3s.; Persian, 8s.; morocco, 10s. 6d. 18mo., 2s. 6d.; Persian, 5s.; calf or morocco, 7s.; gilt, 8s. 6d. 8vo. with borders round pages, Persian calf, 21s.; morocco, 25s. 4to., Illustrated, cloth, 21s.; leather extra, 31s. 6d. Illustrated, morocco, £5 5s.; superior, £6 6s.

Bible History for the use of Schools. By Gilmour. 12mo., 2s.

———————— By a Teacher. Illustrated. 12mo., 5s.

Blessed Lord. *See* Ribadeneira; Rutter (Rev. H.).

Blessed Virgin, Devotions to. From Ancient Sources. *See* Regina Sæculorum. 12mo., 1s. and 3s.

———— Devout Exercise in honour of. From the Psalter and Prayers of S. Bonaventure, 32mo., 1s.

———— History of. By Orsini. Translated by Provost Husenbeth. Illustrated, 12mo., 3s. 6d.

———— Life of. In verse. By C. E. Tame, Esq. 16mo., 2s.

———— Life of. Proposed as a model to Christian women. 12mo., 1s.

———— in North America, Devotion to. By Fr. Macleod. 5s.

———— Veneration of. By Mrs. Stuart Laidlaw. 16mo., 4d.

———— *See* Our Lady, p. 22; Leaflets, p. 16; May, p. 19.

Blindness, Cure of, through the Intercession of Our Lady and S. Ignatius. 12mo., 2d.

BLOSIUS, Spiritual Works of:—The Rule of the Spiritual Life; The Spiritual Mirror; String of Spiritual Jewels. Edited by Rev. Fr. Bowden. 12mo., 3s. 6d.; red edges, 4s.

Blue Scapular, Origin of. 18mo., 1d.

BLYTH (Rev. Fr.), **Devout Paraphrase on the Seven Penitential Psalms**. To which is added "Necessity of Purifying the Soul," by St. Francis de Sales. 18mo., 1s. stronger bound, 1s. 6d.; red edges, 2s.

BONA (Cardinal), **Easy Way to God**. Translated by Father Collins. 12mo., 3s.

BONAVENTURE (S.), **Devout Exercise in honour of Our Lady**. 32mo., 1s.

BONAVENTURE (S.), Life of St. Francis of Assisi. 3s. 6d.
Boniface (S.), Life of. By Mrs. Hope. 12mo., 6s.
BORROMEO (S. Charles), Rules for a Christian Life. 2d.
BOUDON (Mgr.), Book of Perpetual Adoration. Translated by Rev. Dr. Redman. 12mo., 3s.; red edges, 3s. 6d.
BOUDREAUX (Rev. J., S.J.), God our Father. 12mo., 4s.
——— Happiness of Heaven. 12mo., 4s.
——— Paradise of God. 12mo., 4s.
BOURKE (Rev. Ulick J.), Easy Lessons: or, Self-Instruction in Irish. 12mo., 2s. 6d.
BOWDEN (Rev. Fr. John), Spiritual Works of Louis of Blois. 12mo., 3s. 6d.; red edges, 4s.
——— Oratorian Lives of the Saints. (Page 22).
BOWDEN (Mrs.), Lives of the First Religious of the Visitation of Holy Mary. 2 vols., 12mo., 10s.
BOWLES (Emily), Eagle and Dove. Translated from the French of Mdlle. Zénaïde Fleuriot. 12mo., 2s. 6d. and 5s.
BRADBURY (Rev. Fr.), Journey of Sophia and Eulalis to the Palace of True Happiness. 12mo., 1s. 6d.; 3s. 6d.
BRICKLEY'S Standard Table Book. 32mo., ½d.
BRIDGES (Miss), Sir Thomas Maxwell and his Ward. 12mo., 1s. and 2s.
Bridget (S.), Life of, and other Saints of Ireland. 12mo., 1s.
Brigit (S.) Life of, &c. By M. F. Cusack. 8vo., 6s.
Broken Chain. A Tale. 18mo., 6d.
BROWNE (E. G. K., Esq.), Monastic Legends. 8vo., 6d.
BROWNLOW (Rev. W. R. B.), Church of England and its Defenders. 8vo., 1st letter, 6d.; 2nd letter, 1s.
——— "Vitis Mystica"; or, the True Vine: a Treatise on the Passion of our Lord. 18mo., 4s.; red edges, 4s. 6d.
BUCKLEY (Rev. M.), Sermons, Lectures, &c. 12mo., 6s.
BURDER (Abbot), Confidence in the Mercy of God. By Mgr. Languet. 12mo., 3s.
——— The Consoler; or, Pious Readings addressed to the Sick and all who are afflicted. By Père Lambillotte. 12mo., 4s. 6d.; red ed., 5s.
——— Souls in Purgatory. 32mo., 3d.
——— Novena for the Souls in Purgatory. 32mo., 3d.
Burial of the Dead. For Children and Adults. (Latin and English.) Clear type edition, 32mo., 6d.; roan, 1s. 6d.
Burke (Edmund), Life of. See Robertson (Professor).
BURKE (S.H., M.A.), Men and Women of the English Reformation. 12mo., 2 vols., 13s.; Vol. II., 5s.
BURKE (Rev. T. N.), Lectures and Sermons. 2 vols., 24s.
BURKE (Father), and others, Catholic Sermons. 12mo., 2s.
BUTLER (Alban), Lives of the Saints. 2 vols., 8vo., 28s.; gilt, 34s.; 4 vols., 8vo., 32s.; gilt, 50s.; leather, 64s.
——— One Hundred Pious Reflections. 18mo., 1s. and 2s.
BUTLER (Dr.), Catechisms. 1st, ½d.; 2nd, 1d.; 3rd, 1½d.
CALIXTE—Life of the Ven. Anna Maria Taigi. Translated by A. V. Smith Sligo. 8vo., 2s. 6d. and 5s.

R. Washbourne, 18 Paternoster Row, London.

Callista. Dramatised by Dr. Husenbeth. 12mo., 2s.
Captain Rougemont ; or, the Miraculous Conversion. 8vo., 2s. 6d.
CARAHER (Hugh), A Month at Lourdes and its Neighbourhood. Two Illustrations. 12mo., 2s.
Cassilda ; or, the Moorish Princess of Toledo. 8vo., 2s. 6d.
Catechisms—The Catechism of Christian Doctrine. Good large type on superfine paper. 32mo., 1d., cloth, 2d.; interleaved, 8d.
——— The Catechism of Christian Doctrine. Illustrated with passages from the Holy Scriptures. By the Rev. J. B. Bagshawe. 12mo., 2s. 6d.
——— made Easy. By Rev. H. Gibson. Vol. II, 4s.; Vol. III., 4s.
——— Lessons on Christian Doctrine. 18mo., 1½d.
——— General Catechism of the Christian Doctrine. By the Right Rev. Bishop Poirier. 18mo., 9d.
——— By Fr. Power. 3 vols., 10s. 6d. ; 2 vols., 7s. 6d.
——— By Dr. Butler. 32mo., 1st, ½d.; 18mo., 2nd, 1d.; 3rd, 1½d.
——— By Dr. Doyle. 18mo., 1½d.
——— Fleury's Historical. Complete Edition. 18mo., 1½d.
——— Frassinetti's Dogmatic. 12mo., 3s.
——— of the Council. 12mo., 2d.
——— of Perseverance. By Abbé Gaume. 12mo., Vol. I., 7s. 6d.
Catherine Hamilton. By M. F. S. 12mo., 2s. 6d.; gilt, 3s.
Catherine Grown Older. By M. F. S. 12mo., 2s. 6d.; gilt, 3s.
Catholic Hours. See Beste (J. R. Digby).
Catholic Keepsake. A Gift Book for all Seasons. 12mo., 6s.
Catholic Piety. See Prayer Books, page 30.
Catholic Sick and Benefit Club. See Richardson (Rev. R.).
CHALLONER (Bishop), Grounds of Catholic Doctrine Large type edition. 18mo., 4d.
——— Memoirs of Missionary Priests. 8vo., 6s.
——— Think Well on't. 18mo., 2d.; cloth, 6d.
CHAMBERS (F.), The Fair Maid of Kent. 8vo., 6d.
CHARDON (Abbe), Memoirs of a Guardian Angel. 4s.
Chats about the Rosary. See Aunt Margaret's Little Neighbours.
CHAUGY (Mother Frances Magdalen de), Lives of the First Religious of the Visitation. 2 vols., 12mo., 10s.
Child (The). See Dupanloup (Mgr.).
Child's Book of the Passion of Our Lord. 32mo., 6d.
Child (The) of Mary's Manual. Second edition, 32mo. 1s.
Children of Mary in the World, Association of. 32mo., 1d.
Choir, Catholic, Manual. By C. B. Lyons. 12mo., 1s.
Christ bearing His Cross. A Steel Engraving from the Picture miraculously given to Blessed Colomba, with a short account of her Life. 8vo., 6d.; proofs, 1s.
CHRISTIAN BROTHERS' Reading Books.
Christian Doctrine, Lessons on. 18mo., 1½d.
Christian, Duties of a. By Ven. de la Salle. 12mo., 2s
Christian Politeness. By the same Author. 18mo., 1s.
Christian Teacher. By the same Author. 18mo., 1s. 8d.
Christmas Offering. 32mo., 1s. a 100 ; or 7s. 6d. for 1000.
Christmas (The First) for our dear Little Ones. 4to., 5s.

Chronological Sketches. *See* Murray Lane (H.).
Church Defence. *See* Marshall (T. W. M.).
Church History. By Alzog. 8vo., 3 vols. each 20s.
——————— By Darras. 4 vols., 8vo., 48s.
——————— Compendium. By Noethen. 12mo., 8s.
——————— for Schools. By Noethen. 12mo., 5s. 6d.
Church of England and its Defenders. *See* Brownlow (Rev.).
Cistercian Legends of the XIII. Century. *See* Collins (Fr.).
Cistercian Order: its Mission and Spirit. *See* Collins (Fr.).
Civilization and the See of Rome. *See* Montagu (Lord).
Clare (Sister Mary Cherubini) of S. Francis, Life of. Preface by Lady Herbert. With Portrait. 12mo., 3s. 6d.
Cloister Legends; or, Convents and Monasteries in the Older Time. 12mo., 4s.
COGERY (A.), Third French Course, with Vocabulary. 12mo., 2s.
COLLINS (Rev. Fr.), Cistercian Legends of the XIII. Century. 12mo., 3s. [3s. 6d.
——————— Cistercian Order: its Mission and Spirit. 12mo.,
——————— Easy Way to God. Translated from the Latin of Cardinal Bona. 12mo., 3s.
——————— Spiritual Conferences on the Mysteries of Faith and the Interior Life. 12mo., 5s.
COLOMBIERE (Father Claude de la), The Sufferings of Our Lord. Sermons preached in the Chapel Royal, St. James's, in the year 1677. Preface by Fr. Doyotte, S.J. 18mo., 1s.; stronger bound, 1s. 6d.; red edges, 2s.
Colombini (B. Giovanni), Life of. By Belcari. Translated from the editions of 1541 and 1832. With Portrait. 12mo., 3s. 6d.
Columba (S.) Life of, &c. By M. F. Cusack. 8vo., 6s.
Columbkille, or Columba (S.), Life and Prophecies of. By St. Adamnan. 12mo., 3s. 6d.
Comedy of Convocation in the English Church. Edited by Archdeacon Chasuble. 8vo., 2s. 6d. *See* page 18.
COMERFORD (Rev. P.), Handbook of the Confraternity of the Sacred Heart. 18mo., 3d.
——————— Month of May for all the Faithful; or, a Practical Life of the Blessed Virgin. 32mo., 1s.
——————— Pleadings of the Sacred Heart. 18mo., 1s.; gilt, 2s.; with the Handbook of the Confraternity, 1s. 6d.
Communion, Prayers for, for Children. Preparation, Mass before Communion, Thanksgiving. 32mo. 1d.
Compendious Statement of the Scripture Doctrine regarding the Nature and chief Attributes of the Kingdom of Christ. By C. F. A. 8vo., 1s.
COMPTON (Herbert), Semi-Tropical Trifles. 12mo., boards, 1s.; extra cloth, 2s. 6d.
Conferences. *See* Collins, Lacordaire, Mermillod, Ravignan.
Confession, Auricular. By Rev. Dr. Melia. 18mo., 1s. 6d.
Confession and Holy Communion: Young Catholic's Guide. By Dr. Kenny. 32mo., 4d.; cloth, 6d.; red edges, 9d.; French morocco, 1s. 6d.; calf or morocco, 2s. 6d.

Confidence in God. By Cardinal Manning. 16mo., 1s.
Confidence in the Mercy of God. By Mgr. Languet. Translated by Abbot Burder. 12mo., 3s.
Confirmation, Instructions for the Sacrament of. A very complete book. 18mo., 3d.
CONSCIENCE (Hendrick), The Amulet. 12mo., 4s.
——— The Conscript and Blind Rosa. 12mo., 4s.
——— Count Hugo, of Graenhove. 12mo., 4s.
——— The Fisherman's Daughter. 12mo., 4s.
——— Happiness of being Rich. 12mo., 4s.
——— Ludovic and Gertrude. 12mo., 4s.
——— The Village Innkeeper. 12mo., 4s.
——— Young Doctor. 12mo., 4s.
Consoler (The). By Abbot Burder. 12mo., 4s. 6d. and 5s.
Contemplations on the Most Holy Sacrament of the Altar; or Devout Meditations to serve as Preparations for, and Thanksgiving after, Communion. Drawn chiefly from the Holy Scriptures. 18mo., 1s. and 2s.; red edges, 2s. 6d.
Continental Fish Cook. By M. J. N. de Frederic. 18mo., 1s.
Conversion of the Teutonic Race. By Mrs. Hope. 2 vols. 10s.
Convert Martyr; or, "Callista." By the Rev. Dr. Newman, Dramatised by the Rev. Dr. Husenbeth. 12mo., 2s.
Convocation, Comedy of. By the Author of "The Oxford Undergraduate of Twenty Years Ago." 8vo. 2s. 6d.
CORTES (John Donoso), Essays on Catholicism, Liberalism, and Socialism. 12mo., 5s.
CRASSET'S Devout Meditations. Translated. 12mo., 8s.
Crests, The Book of Family. Comprising nearly every bearing and its blazonry, Surnames of Bearers, Dictionary of Mottoes, British and Foreign Orders of Knighthood, Glossary of Terms, and upwards of 4,000 Engravings, Illustrative of Peers, Baronets, and nearly every Family bearing Arms in England, Wales, Scotland, Ireland, and the Colonies, &c. 2 vols., 12mo., 24s.
Crucifixion, The. A large Picture for School walls, 1s.
CULPEPPER. Family Herbal, 3s. 6d.; coloured plates, 5s. 6d.
CUSACK (M. F.):—Sister Mary Francis Clare.
 Book of the Blessed Ones. 12mo., 4s. 6d.
 Devotions for Public and Private Use at the Way of the Cross. Illustrated. 32mo., 1s.; red edges, 1s. 6d.
 Father Matthew, Life of. 12mo., 2s. 6d.
 Good Reading for Sundays and Festivals. 2s. 6d.
 Ireland, Patriot's History of. 18mo., 2s.
 Jesus and Jerusalem; or, the Way Home. 12mo., 4s. 6d.
 Joseph (S.), Life of. 32mo., 1s.
 Life of the Most Rev. Dr. Dixon. 12mo., 7s. 6d.
 Lives of St. Columba and St. Brigit. 8vo., 6s.
 Mary O'Hagan, Abbess, Life of. 8vo., 6s.
 Memorare Mass. 32mo., 2d.
 Ned Rusheen. 12mo., 5s.
 Nun's Advice to her Girls. 12mo., 2s. 6d.
 O'Connell; his Life and Times. 2 vols. 8vo., 18s.

Patrick (S.), Life of. 8vo., 6s., gilt, 10s.; 32mo., 1s.
    Illustrated by Doyle (large edition), 4to., 20s.
Patrick's (S.) Manual. 18mo., 3s. 6d.
Pilgrim's Way to Heaven. 12mo., 4s. 6d.
Stations of the Cross, for Public and Private Use.
    Illustrated. 16mo., 1s.; red edges, 1s. 6d.
The Liberator; his Public Speeches and Letters.
    2 vols. 8vo., 18s.
The Spouse of Christ. 12mo., vol. 2, 7s. 6d.
Tim O'Halloran's Choice. 12mo., 3s. 6d.
Tronson's Conferences. 12mo., 4s. 6d.

DARRAS (Abbe), History of the Church. 4 vols., 8vo., 48s.
Daughter (A) of S. Dominick: (Bells of the Sanctuary). By Grace Ramsay. 12mo., 1s. and 1s. 6d.; better bound, 2s.
DAVIS (F.), Earlier and Later Leaves; or, an Autumn Gathering. Poems and Songs. 12mo., 6s.
DAVIS (Rev. R. G.) Garden of the Soul. *See* pages 30 and 32.
DEAN (Rev. J. Joy), Devotion to Sacred Heart. 12mo., 2s.
DECHAMPS (Mgr.), The Life of Pleasure. 12mo., 1s. 6d.
DE DOSS (P. A., S.J.), The Pearl among the Virtues; 3s.
Defence of the Roman Church. *See* Gueranger.
DEHAM (Rev. F.) Sacred Heart of Jesus, offered to the Piety of the Young engaged in Study. 32mo., 6d.
Diary of a Confessor of the Faith. 12mo., 1s.
Directorium Asceticum. By Scaramelli. 4 vols., 12mo., 24s.
DIXON (Fr., O.P.) Albert the Great: his Life and Scholastic Labours. From original documents. By Dr. Sighart. With Photographic Portrait. 8vo. 10s. 6d. Cheap edition, 5s.
——— Life of St. Vincent Ferrer. From the French of Rev. Fr. Pradel. With a Photograph. 12mo., 5s.
DOYLE (Canon, O.S.B.), Life of Gregory Lopez, the Hermit. With a Photographic Portrait. 12mo., 3s. 6d.
DOYLE (Dr.), Catechism. 18mo., 1½d.
DOYOTTE (Rev. Fr., S.J.), Elevations to the Heart of Jesus. 12mo., 3s.
——— Sufferings of Our Lord. *See* Columbiere (Fr.)
DRAMAS, &c.—Convert Martyr; or, "Callista" dramatised. 2s.
——— The Duchess Transformed. By W. H. A. (Girls, 1 Act). A Comedy. 12mo., 6d.
——— Ernscliff Hall (Girls, 3 Acts). Drama. 12mo., 6d.
——— Filiola (Girls, 4 Acts). Drama. 12mo., 6d.
——— He would be a Lord (Boys, 3 Acts), a Comedy. 2s.
——— He would be a Soldier (Boys, 2 Acts), Comedy, 6d.
——— Major John Andre [Historical] (Boys, 5 Acts), 2s.
——— Reverse of the Medal (Girls, 4 Acts). Drama. 6d.
——— Shandy Maguire (Boys, 2 Acts), a Farce. 12mo., 2s.
——— St. Eustace (Boys, 5 Acts). Drama. 12mo., 1s.
——— St. Louis in Chains (Boys, 5 Acts). Drama. 12mo., 2s.
——— St. William of York (Boys, 2 Acts). Drama. 12mo., 6d.
——— Whittington and his Cat. Drama for Children. 9 Scenes. By Henrietta Fairfield. 6d.
——— *See* Shakespeare.

Duchess (The), Transformed. By W. H. A. 12mo., 6d.
DUMESNIL (Abbe), Recollections of the Reign of Terror. 12mo., 2s. 6d.
DUPANLOUP (Mgr.), Contemporary Prophecies. 8vo., 1s.
────── The Child. Translated by Kate Anderson. 12mo., 3s. 6d.
Dusseldorf Gallery. 357 Engravings. Large 4to. Half-morocco, gilt, £5 5s. nett.
────── 134 Engravings. Large 8vo. Half-morocco, gilt, 42s.
Dusseldorf Society for the Distribution of Good Religious Pictures. Subscription, 8s. 6d. a year. *Catalogue* 3d.
Duties of a Christian. By Ven. de la Salle. 12mo., 2s.
Eagle and Dove. *See* Bowles (Emily).
E. A. M. Countess Adelstan. 12mo., 1s. and 2s. 6d.
────── Paul Seigneret. 12mo., 6d., 1s., 1s. 6d., gilt, 2s.
────── Regina Sæculorum. 12mo., 1s. and 3s.
────── Rosalie. 12mo., 1s., 1s. 6d., gilt, 2s.
Easy Way to God. By Cardinal Bona. 12mo., 3s.
Ebba; or, the Supernatural Power of the Blessed Sacrament. *This book is in French.* 12mo., 1s. 6d.; cloth, 2s. 6d.
Electricity and Magnetism; an Enquiry into the Nature and Results of. By Amyclanus. Illustrated. 12mo., 6s. 6d.
England, History of. *See* Evans.
Epistles and Gospels. Good clear type edition, 32mo., 6d.; roan, 1s. 6d.; larger edition, 18mo., French morocco, 2s.
──────, Explanation of. By Rev. F. Goffine. Illustrated, 8vo., 9s.
Epistles of S. Paul, Exposition of. *See* MacEvilly (Rt. Rev. Dr.)
Ernscliff Hall. A Drama in Three Acts, for Girls. 12mo., 6d.
Eucharistic Year. 18mo., 4s.
Eucharist (The) and the Christian Life. *See* La Bouillerie.
Europe, Modern, History of. With Preface by Bishop Weathers. 12mo., 5s.; roan, 5s. 6d.; cloth gilt, 6s.
Eustace (St.). A Drama in 5 Acts for Boys. By Rev. T. Meyrick, M.A. 12mo., 1s.
EVANS (L.), History of England, adapted for Junior Classes in Schools. 9d., or separately: Part 1 (Standard 4) 2d. Part 2 (Standard 4) 2d. Part 3 (Standard 5) 3d.
────── Chronological Outline of English History. 1½d.
────── Milton's l'Allegro (Oxford Local Exam.). 2d.
────── Parsing and Analysis Table. 1d.
FAIRFIELD (Henrietta), Whittington and his Cat. A Drama, in 9 Scenes, for Children. 12mo., 6d.
Fairy Ching (The); or, the Chinese Fairies' Visit to England. By Henrica Frederic. 12mo., 1s.; gilt edges, 1s. 6d.
Fairy Tales for Little Children. By Madeleine Howley Meehan. 12mo., 6d.; stronger bound, 1s. and 1s. 6d.; gilt, 2s.
Faith of Our Fathers. *See* Gibbons (Most Rev. Archbishop).
Fall, Redemption, and Exaltation of Man. 12mo., 1s.
Familiar Instructions on Christian Truths. By a Priest. 12mo., 10d.
FARRELL (Rev. J.), Lectures of a certain Professor. 7s. 6d.
FAVRE (Abbe), Heaven Opened by the Practice of Frequent Confession and Communion. 12mo., 2s.; stronger bound, 3s. 6d.; red edges, 4s.

Feasts (The) of Camelot, with the Tales that were told there. By Mrs. T. K. Hervey. 12mo., 3s. 6d., or in 2 vols. 1s. each.
FERRIS (Rev. D.), Life of St. Mary Frances of the Five Wounds of Jesus Christ. From the Italian. 12mo., 3s. 6d.
Filiola. A Drama in Four Acts, for Girls. 12mo., 6d.
First Apostles of Europe. *See* Hope (Mrs.).
First Communion and Confirmation Memorial. Beautifully printed in gold and colours, folio, 1s. each, or 9s. a dozen, nett.
First Religious of the Visitation of Holy Mary, Lives of. With two Photographs. 2 vols., 12mo., 10s.
FLEET (Charles). Tales and Sketches. 8vo., 2s.; stronger bound, 2s. 6d.; gilt, 3s. 6d.
FLEURIOT (Mlle. Zenaide), Eagle and Dove. Translated by Emily Bowles. 12mo., 2s. 6d. and 5s.
FLEURY'S Historical Catechism. Large edition, 12mo., 1½d.
Flowers of Christian Wisdom. *See* Henry (Lucien).
Fluffy. A Tale for Boys. By M. F. S. 12mo., 3s. 6d.
Following of Christ. *See* A'Kempis.
Foreign Books. *See* R. W.'s Catalogue of Foreign Books. 3d.
Francis of Assisi (S.) Life of. By S. Bonaventure. Translated by Miss Lockhart. 12mo., 3s. 6d.
FRANCIS OF SALES (S.), Consoling Thoughts. 18mo., 2s.
———— The Mystical Flora; or, the Christian Life under the Emblem of Saints. 4to., 8s.
———— Necessity of Purifying the Soul. *See* Blyth (Rev. Fr.).
———— Sweetness of Holy Living. 18mo., 1s.; levant, 3s.
Franciscan Annals and Monthly Bulletin of the Third Order of St. Francis. 8vo., 6d.
FRANCO (Rev. S.) Devotions to the Sacred Heart. 12mo., 4s.; cheap edition, 2s.
FRASSINETTI—Dogmatic Catechism. 12mo., 3s.
FREDERIC (Henrica), The Fairy Ching; or, the Chinese Fairies' Visit to England. 12mo., 1s.; gilt edges, 1s. 6d.
FREDERIC (M. J. N. de), Continental Fish Cook; or, a Few Hints on Maigre Dinners. 18mo., 1s., soiled covers, 6d.
Freemasons, Irish and English, and their Foreign Brothers. 4to., 2s.
From Sunrise to Sunset. By L. B. 12mo., 3s. 6d.
GALLERY (Rev. D.), Handbook of Essentials in History and Literature, Ancient and Modern. 18mo., 1s.
Garden of the Soul. *See* page 32.
Garden (Little) of the Soul. *See* page 30.
Gathered Gems from Spanish Authors. *See* Monteiro.
GAUME (Abbe), Catechism of Perseverance. 4 vols., 12mo. Vol. 1, 7s. 6d.
GAYRARD (Mme. Paul) Harmony of the Passion. Compiled from the four Gospels, in Latin and French. 18mo., 1s. 6d.
German (S.), Life of. 12mo., 3s. 6d.
GIBBONS (Most Rev. Archbishop), The Faith of Our Fathers; Being a Plain Exposition and Vindication of the Church Founded by our Lord Jesus Christ. 12mo., 4s. Paper covers, 2s.

R. Washbourne, 18 Paternoster Row, London.

GIBSON (Rev. H.), Catechism made Easy. 12mo., Vol. I. (out of print); Vol. II., 4s.; Vol. III., 4s.
GILMOUR (Rev. R.), Bible History for the Use of Schools. Illustrated. 12mo., 2s.
God our Father. By a Father of the Society of Jesus. 12mo., 4s.
GOFFINE (Rev. F.), Explanation of the Epistles and Gospels. Illustrated. 8vo., 9s.
Good Thoughts for Priests and People. *See* Noethen.
Gospels, An Exposition of. *See* MacEvilly (Most Rev. Dr.).
Grace before and after Meals. 32mo., 1d.; cloth, 2d.
GRACE RAMSAY. A Daughter of S. Dominick (Bells of the Sanctuary, No. 4). 12mo., 1s.; stronger bound, 1s. 6d. and 2s.
——— *See* O'Meara (Kathleen).
GRACIAN (Fr. Baltasar), Sanctuary Meditations for Priests and Frequent Communicants. Translated from the Spanish by Mariana Monteiro. 12mo., 4s.
Grains of Gold. Counsels for the Sanctification and Happiness of Life. 16mo., Series 1 and 2, cloth, 2s. 6d.
GRANT (Bishop), Pastoral on St. Joseph. 32mo., 4d. & 6d.
Gregorian, or Plain Chant and Modern Music. 8vo., 2s. 6d.
Gregory Lopez, the Hermit, Life of. By Canon Doyle, O.S.B. With a Photographic Portrait. 12mo., 3s. 6d.
Grounds of the Catholic Doctrine. By Bishop Challoner. Large type edition, 18mo., 4d.
Guardian Angel, Memoirs of a. By Abbé Chardon. 12mo., 4s.
GUERANGER (Dom), Defence of the Roman Church against F. Gratry. Translated by Canon Woods. 8vo., 1s.
Guide to Sacred Eloquence. *See* Passionist Fathers.
HALL (E.), Munster Firesides. 12mo., 3s. 6d.
Happiness of Being Rich. By Conscience. 12mo., 4s.
Happiness of Heaven. By a Father of the Society of Jesus. 12mo. 4s.
Harmony of Anglicanism. By T. W. Marshall. 8vo., 2s. 6d.
HAY (Bishop), Sincere Christian. 18mo., 2s. 6d.
——— Devout Christian. 18mo., 2s. 6d.
He would be a Lord. A Comedy in 3 Acts. (Boys). 12mo., 2s.
Heaven Opened by the Practice of frequent Confession and Holy Communion. By the Abbé Favre. 12mo., 2s.; stronger bound, 3s. 6d.; red edges, 4s.
HEDLEY (Bishop), Five Sermons—Light of the Holy Spirit in the World. 12mo., 1s.; cloth, 1s. 6d. Revelation, Mystery, Dogma and Creeds, Infallibility: separately, 3d. each.
HEIGHAM (John), A Devout Exposition of the Holy Mass. Edited by Austin John Rowley, Priest. 12mo., 4s.
Henri V. (Comte de Chambord). *See* Walsh (W. H.).
HENRY (Lucien), Flowers of Christian Wisdom. 18mo., 1s. and 2s.; red edges, 2s. 6d.
Herbal, Brook's Family. 12mo., 3s. 6d.; coloured plates, 5s. 6d.
HERBERT (Wallace), My Dream and Verses Miscellaneous. With a frontispiece. 12mo., 5s.
——— The Angels and the Sacraments. 16mo., 1s.

HERGENRÖTHER (Dr.), **Anti-Janus.** Translated by Professor Robertson. 12mo., 6s.
HERVEY (Eleanora Louisa), **My Godmother's Stories from many Lands.** 12mo., 3s. 6d.
——— **Our Legends and Lives.** 12mo., 6s.
——— **Rest on the Cross.** 12mo., 3s. 6d.
——— **The Feasts of Camelot, with the Tales that were told there.** 12mo., 3s. 6d. ; or, separately: Christmas 1s. ; Whitsuntide, 1s.
HILL (Rev. Fr.), **Elements of Philosophy,** comprising Logic and General Principles of Metaphysics. 8vo., 6s.
HOFFMAN (Franz), **Industry and Laziness.** 12mo., 3s.
Holy Childhood. A book of simple Prayers and Instructions for very little children. 32mo., 6d. or 1s. ; gilt, 1s. 6d.
Holy Church the Centre of Unity. *See* Shaw (T. H.)
Holy Communion. By Hubert Lebon. 12mo., 4s.
Holy Family, Confraternity of. *See* Manning (Card.).
Holy Places: their Sanctity and Authenticity. *See* Philpin.
Holy Readings. *See* Beste (J. R. Digby Esq.).
HOPE (Mrs.), **The First Apostles of Europe** ; or, "The Conversion of the Teutonic Race." 2 vols., 12mo., 10s.
Horace. Literally translated by Smart. 18mo., 2s.
HUGUET (Pere), **The Power of S. Joseph.** Meditations and Devotions. Translated by Clara Mulholland. 1s. 6d.
HUMPHREY (Rev. W., S.J.), **The Panegyrics of Fr. Segneri, S.J.** Translated from the orignal Italian. With a Preface by the Rev. W. Humphrey, S.J. 12mo., 5s.
HUSENBETH (Rev. Dr.), **Convert Martyr.** 12mo., 2s.
——— **History of the Blessed Virgin.** Translated from Orsini. Illustrated. 12mo., 3s. 6d.
——— **Life and Sufferings of Our Lord.** By Rev. H. Rutter. Illustrated. 12mo., 5s.
——— **Life of Mgr. Weedall.** 8vo., 1s.
——— **Little Office of the Immaculate Conception.** In Latin and English. 32mo., 4d. ; cloth, 6d.; roan, 1s. ; calf or morocco, 2s. 6d.
——— **Our Blessed Lady of Lourdes.** 18mo., 6d.; with the Novena, 1s.; cloth, 1s. 6d. Novena, separately, 4d.; Litany, 1d.
——— **Roman Question.** 8vo., 6d.
Husenbeth (Provost), **Sermon on his Death.** By Very Rev. Canon Dalton. 8vo. 6d.
HUTCH (Rev. W., D D.), **Nano Nangle,** her Life and her Labours. 12mo., 7s. 6d.
Hymn Book (The Catholic). Edited by Rev. G. L. Vere. 32mo., 2d.; cloth, 4d.; Appendix (Hymns to Saints), 1d.
Iceland (Three Sketches of Life in). By Carl Andersen. 12mo.
IGNATIUS (S.), **Spiritual Exercises.** By Fr. Bellecio, S.J. Translated by Dr. Hutch. 18mo., 2s.
Ignatius (S.), **Cure of Blindness through the Intercession of Our Lady and S. Ignatius.** 12mo., 2d.

Imitation of Christ. *See* A'Kempis.
Immaculate Conception, Definition of. 12mo., 6d.
—————— Little Office of. *See* Husenbeth (Rev. Dr.).
—————— Little Office of, in Latin and English. 32mo., 1d.
Indulgences. *See* Maurel (Rev. F. A.).
Industry and Laziness. By Franz Hoffman. From the German, by James King. 12mo., 3s.
Infallibility of the Pope. By the Author of "The Oxford Undergraduate of Twenty Years Ago." 8vo., 1s.
In Suffragiis Sanctorum. Commem. S. Josephi; Commem. S. Georgii. Set of 5 for 4d.
Insurrection of '98. By Rev. P. F. Kavanagh. 12mo., 2s. 6d.
IOTA. The Adventures of a Protestant in Search of a Religion: being the Story of a late Student of Divinity at Bunyan Baptist College; a Nonconformist Minister, who seceded to the Catholic Church. 12mo., 3s. 6d.; cheap edition, 2s.
Ireland (History of). By Miss Cusack. 18mo., 2s. A larger edition, illustrated by Doyle, 8vo., 11s.
Ireland (History of). By T. Young. 18mo., 2s. 6d.
Ireland Ninety Years ago. 12mo., 1s.
Ireland, Popular Poetry of. (Songs). 262 pages, 18mo., 6d.
Ireland, Revelations of, in the Past Generation. 12mo. 1s.
Irish Board Reading Books.
Irish First Book. 18mo., 2d. Second Book. 18mo., 4d.
Irish Monthly. 8vo. Vol. 1877, cloth, 8s.
Italian Revolution (The History of). The History of the Barricades. By Keyes O'Clery, M.P. 8vo., 7s. 6d. and 3s. 6d.
JACOB (W. J.), Personal Recollections of Rome. 6d.
JENKINS (Rev. O. L.) Student's Handbook of British and American Literature. 12mo., 8s.
Jesuits (The), and other Essays. *See* Nevin (Willis, Esq.)
Jesus and Jerusalem; or, the Way Home. *See* Cusack (Miss).
John of God (S.), Life of. With Photographic Portrait. 12mo., 5s.
Joseph (S.), Life of. By Miss Cusack. 32mo., 6d.; cloth, 1s.
—————— Novena of Meditations. 18mo., 1s.
—————— Novena to, with a Pastoral by the late Bishop Grant. 32mo., 4d.; cloth, 6d.
—————— Power of. *See* Huguet.
—————— *See* Leaflets.
Journey of Sophia and Eulalie to the Palace of True Happiness. From the French by Rev. Fr. Bradbury. 12mo., 1s. 6d.; better bound, 3s. 6d.
KAVANAGH (Rev. P. F.), Insurrection of '98. 1s. 6d.
Keighley Hall, and other Tales. By E. King. 18mo., 6d.; cloth, 1s.; stronger bound, 1s. 6d.; gilt, 2s.
KEMEN (Charles), The Marpingen Apparitions. 8vo., 1s.
KENNY (Dr.), Young Catholic's Guide to Confession and Holy Communion. 32mo., 4d.; cloth, 6d.; red edges, 9d.; roan, 1s. 6d.; calf or morocco, 2s. 6d.

R. Washbourne, 18 *Paternoster Row, London.*

KENNY (Dr.), New Year's Gift to our Heavenly Father. 32mo., 4d.
KERNEY (M. T.), Compendium of History. 12mo., 5s.
Key of Heaven. *See* Prayers, page 31.
KINANE (Rev. T. H.), Dove of the Tabernacle. 1s. 6d.
——— Angel (The) of the Altar; or, the Love of the Most Adorable and Most Sacred Heart of Jesus. 18mo., 2s. 3d.
——— Mary Immaculate, Mother of God; or Devotions in honour of the B. V. M. 18mo., 2s.
KING (Elizabeth), Keighley Hall, and other Tales. 18mo., 6d.; cloth, 1s.; stronger bound, 1s. 6d.; gilt, 2s.
——— The Silver Teapot. 18mo., 4d.
KING (James). Industry and Laziness. 12mo., 3s.
Kishoge Papers. Tales of Devilry and Drollery. 12mo., 1s. 6d.
LA BOUILLERIE (Mgr. de), The Eucharist and the Christian Life. Translated by L. C. 12mo., 3s. 6d.
LACORDAIRE'S Conferences. 12mo., On Life, 3s. 6d.; God, 6s.; Jesus Christ, 6s.
Lacordaire. The Inner Life of Pere Lacordaire. From the French of Père Chocarne. 12mo., 6s. 6d.
Lady Mildred's Housekeeper, A Few Words from. 2d.
LAIDLAW (Mrs. Stuart), Letters to my God-child. No. 4. On the Veneration of the Blessed Virgin. 16mo., 4d.
LAING (Rev. Dr.), Blessed Virgin's Root traced in the Tribe of Ephraim. 8vo., 10s. 6d.
——— Descriptive Guide to the Mass. 12mo., 1s. and 1s. 6d.
——— Knight of the Faith. 12mo., 4s.
 Absurd Protestant Opinions concerning *Intention*. 4d.
 Catholic, not Roman Catholic. 4d.
 Challenge to the Churches. 1d.
 Favourite Fallacy about Private Judgment and Inquiry. 1d.
 Protestantism against the Natural Moral Law. 1d.
 What is Christianity? 6d.
 Whence does the Monarch get his right to Rule? 2s. 6d.
LAMBILOTTE (Pere), The Consoler. Translated by Abbot Burder. 12mo., 4s. 6d.; red edges, 5s.
LANGUET (Mgr.), Confidence in the Mercy of God. Translated by Abbot Burder. 12mo., 3s.
Last of the Catholic O'Malleys. By M. Taunton. 18mo., 1s. 6d.; stronger bound, 2s.
Leaflets. 1d. each, or 1s. 2d. per 100 post free.
 Act of Reparation to the Sacred Heart.
 Archconfraternity of the Agonising Heart of Jesus and the Compassionate Heart of Mary: Prayers for the Dying.
 Archconfraternity of Our Lady of Angels.
 Ditto, Rules.
 Christmas Offering (or 7s. 6d. per 1000).
 Devotions to S. Joseph.
 Gospel according to S. John, *in Latin*. 1s. 6d. per 100.
 Indulgenced Prayers for Souls in Purgatory.

Indulgences attached to Medals, Crosses, Statues, &c., by the Blessing of His Holiness and of those privileged to give his Blessing.
Intentions for Indulgences.
Litany of Our Lady of Angels.
Litany of S. Joseph, and Devotions.
Litany of Resignation.
Miraculous Prayer—August Queen of Angels.
Picture of Crucifixion, "I thirst" (or 5s. a 1000).
Prayer for One's Confessor.
Union of our Life with the Passion of our Lord.
Visit to the Blessed Sacrament. 2s. 6d. per 100.

Leaflets. 1d. each, or 6s. per 100.
Acts of Consecration to the Sacred Heart.
Concise Portrait of the Blessed Virgin.
Explanation of the Medal or Cross of St. Benedict.
Indulgenced Prayers for the Rosary of the Holy Souls.
Indulgenced Prayer before a Crucifix.
Litany of the Seven Dolours.
Prayer to S. Philip Neri.
Prayers before and after Holy Communion.
Revelation made by the mouth of our Saviour to S. Bridget.

LEBON (Hubert), Holy Communion. 12mo., 4s.
Legends of the Saints. By M. F. S. 16mo., 3s. 6d.
Lenten Thoughts. By Bishop Amherst. 18mo., 2s.; red edges, 2s. 6d.
LEO XIII., The Church and Civilisation. 8vo., 2s.
Letter to George Augustus Simcox. 8vo., 6d.
Letters to my God-child. By Mrs. Stuart Laidlaw. 16mo., 4d.
Life in the Cloister. By Miss Stewart. 12mo., 3s. 6d.
Life of Pleasure. By Mgr. Dechamps. 12mo., 1s. 6d.
Light of the Holy Spirit in the World. Five Sermons by Bishop Hedley. 12mo., 1s.; cloth, 1s. 6d.
LIGUORI (S.), Fourteen Stations of the Cross. 18mo., 1d.
——— Selva; or, a Collection of Matter for Sermons. 12mo., 5s.
——— Way of Salvation. 32mo., 1s.
——— Life of. 12mo., 10s.
——— Officium Parvum. Latin and English. With Novena. 12mo., 1s.; cloth, 2s.; red edges, 3s.
Lily of S. Joseph: A little Manual of Prayers and Hymns for Mass. 64mo., 2d.; cloth, 3d., 4d., and 6d.; gilt, 8d.; roan, 1s.; French morocco, 1s. 6d.; calf or morocco, 2s.; gilt, 2s. 6d.
Literature, Philosophy of, An Essay contributing to a. By B. A. M. 12mo., 6s.
Literature, Student's Handbook. See Jenkins (Rev. O. L.).
Little Prayer Book. 32mo., 3d.
Lives of the First Religious of the Visitation of Holy Mary. By Mother Frances Magdalen de Chaugy. With Two Photographs. 2 vols., 12mo., 10s.
Lost Children of Mount St. Bernard. 18mo., 6d.
Louis (S.) in Chains. Drama, Five Acts (Boys). 12mo., 2s.

Lourdes, Our Blessed Lady of. By Rev. Dr. Husenbeth. 18mo., 6d.; with the Novena, 1s.; cloth, 1s. 6d.
———— Novena of, for the use of the Sick. 4d.
———— Litany of. 1d. each.
———— Month at Lourdes. By H. Caraher. 2s.
———— Photograph, Carte de Visite, 1s.
Ludovic and Gertrude. By Conscience. 12mo., 4s.
LUCK (Dom Edmund J.), Short Meditations for every Day in the Year. From the Italian. 12mo. Edition for the Regular Clergy, 2 vols., 9s.; edition for the Secular Clergy and others, 2 vols., 9s.
LYONS (C. B.), Catholic Choir Manual. 12mo., 1s.
———— Catholic Psalmist. 12mo., 4s. [18mo., 2s.
MACDANIEL (M. A.), Month of May for Interior Souls.
———— Novena to S. Joseph. 32mo., 4d.; cloth, 6d.
———— Road to Heaven. A Game. 3s. 6d.
MACEVILLY (Bishop), Exposition of the Epistles of St. Paul and of the Catholic Epistles. 2 vols., large 8vo. 18s.
———— Exposition of the Gospels. Large 8vo., Vol. I., 12s. 6d.
MACLEOD (Rev. X. D.), Devotion to Our Lady in North America. 8vo., 5s.
Major John Andre. An Historical Drama for Boys. Five Acts. 2s.
MANNING (Cardinal), Church, Spirit and the Word. 6d.
———— Confidence in God. 16mo., 1s.
———— Confraternity of the Holy Family. 8vo., 3d.
———— Glory of S. Vincent de Paul. 12mo., 1s.
———— Independence of the Holy See. 12mo., 5s.
———— True Story of the Vatican Council. 12mo., 5s.
MANNOCK (Patrick), Origin and Progress of Religious Orders, and Happiness of a Religious State. Translated from the Latin of Rev. F. Platus. 12mo., 2s. 6d.
Manual of Catholic Devotions. *See* Prayers, page 31.
Manual of Devotions in honour of Our Lady of Sorrows. Compiled by the Clergy at St. Patrick's, Soho. 18mo., 1s. & 1s. 6d.
Manual of the Sisters of Charity. 18mo., 6s.
Margarethe Verflassen. Translated from the German by Mrs. Smith Sligo. 12mo., 1s. 6d. and 3s.; gilt, 3s. 6d.
Margaret Roper. By A. M. Stewart. 12mo., 6s.; extra, 7s.
Marpingen Apparitions. By C. Kemen. 8vo., 1s.
MARQUIGNY (Pere), Life and Letters of Countess Adelstan. 12mo., 1s. and 2s. 6d.
MARSHALL (A. J. P., Esq.), Comedy of Convocation in the English Church. 8vo., 2s. 6d. *
———— English Religion. 8vo. 6d.,
———— Infallibility of the Pope. 8vo., 1s. *
———— Oxford Undergraduate of Twenty Years Ago. 8vo., 2s. 6d.; cloth, 3s. 6d. *
———— Reply to the Bishop of Ripon's Attack on the Catholic Church. 8vo., 6d. *
MARSHALL (T. W. M., Esq.), Harmony of Anglicanism—Church Defence. 8vo., 2s. 6d. *

The 5 (*) in one Volume, 8vo., 6s.

R. Washbourne, 18 Paternoster Row, London.

MARSHALL (Rev. W.), The Doctrine of Purgatory. 1s.
MARTIN (Rev. E. R.), Rule of the Pope-King. 8vo., 6d.
Mary, A Remembrance of. 32mo., 2s.
Mary Christina of Savoy (Venerable). 18mo., 6d.
Mary Immaculate, Devotion to. By Rev. T. H. Kinane. 2s.
Mass, Descriptive Guide to. By Rev. Dr. Laing. 12mo., 1s., or stronger bound, 1s. 6d.
Mass, Devotions for. Very *Large type*, 18mo., 2d.
Mass (The). *See* Müller (Rev. M.), Tronson (Abbe).
Mass, A Devout Exposition of. *See* Rowley (Rev. A. J.).
MATIGNON (Pere) The Duties of Christian Parents. 5s.
MAUREL (Rev. F. A.), Christian Instructed in the Nature and Use of Indulgences. 18mo., 2s.
Maxims of the Kingdom of Heaven. 12mo., 5s.; red edges, 5s. 6d.; calf or mor., 10s. 6d. Old Testament, 1s. 6d.; Gospels, 1s.
May, Month of. By Rev. P. Comerford. 32mo., 1s.
May, Month of. By M. A. Macdaniel. 18mo., 2s.
May, Month of, principally for the use of Religious. 18mo., 1s. 6d.
May Readings for the Feasts of Our Lady. By Rev. A. P. Bethell. 18mo., 1s. 6d.
M'CORRY (Rev. Dr.), Monks of Iona and the Duke of Argyll. 8vo., 3s. 6d.
———— Rome, Past, Present, Future. 8vo., 6d.
MEEHAN (M. H.), Fairy Tales for Little Children. 12mo., 6d. and 1s.; stronger bound, 1s. 6d.; gilt, 2s.
MELIA (Rev. Dr.), Auricular Confession. 18mo., 1s. 6d.
MERMILLOD (Mgr.), The Supernatural Life. Translated from the French, with a Preface by Lady Herbert. 12mo., 5s.
MEYRICK (Rev. T.), Life of St. Wenefred. 12mo., 2s.
———— Lives of the Early Popes. St. Peter to St. Sylvester. 8vo., 4s. 6d.
———— St. Eustace. A Drama (5 Acts) for Boys. 12mo., 1s.
M. F. S., Catherine Hamilton. 12mo., 2s. 6d.; gilt, 3s.
———— Catherine Grown Older. 12mo., 2s. 6d.; gilt, 3s.
———— Fluffy. A Tale for Boys. 12mo., 3s. 6d.
———— Legends of the Saints. 16mo., 3s. 6d. [gilt, 1s. 6d.
———— My Golden Days. 12mo., 2s. 6d.; or in 3 vols., 1s. ea.
———— Stories of Holy Lives. 12mo., 3s. 6d.
———— Stories of Martyr Priests. 12mo., 3s. 6d.
———— Stories of the Saints. 12mo., 3s. 6d.; gilt, 4s. 6d.
———— ———— Second Series. 12mo., 3s. 6d.; gilt, 4s. 6d.
———— ———— Third Series. 12mo., 3s. 6d.
———— Story of the Life of S. Paul. 12mo., 2s. 6d.
———— The Three Wishes. A Tale. 12mo., 2s. 6d.
———— Tom's Crucifix, and other Tales. 12mo., 3s., or in 5 vols., 1s. each, gilt 1s. 6d.
Message from the Mother Heart of Mary. 18mo., 4d. and 6d.
MILES (G. H.), Truce of God. A Tale. 12mo., 4s.
MILNER (Bishop), Devotion to the Sacred Heart of Jesus. 32mo., 3d.; cloth, 6d.; gilt, 1s.

Miracles. A New Miracle at Rome, through the intercession of B. John Berchmans. 12mo., 2d.
——— Cure of Blindness, through the intercession of Our Lady and S. Ignatius. 12mo., 2d.
Mirror of Faith—your Likeness in It. By Fr. Hooker. 3s.
Misgivings—Convictions. 12mo., 6d.
Missal. *See* Prayers, page 31.
Monastic Legends. By E. G. K. Browne. 8vo., 6d.
MOHR (Rev. J., S.J.), Cantiones Sacrae. Hymns and Chants. Music and Words. 8vo., 5s. [2s. 6d.
——— Manual of Sacred Chant. Music and Words. 18mo.
MONK (Rev. Fr., O.S.B.), Daily Exercises. 18mo., 3s. 6d.
Monk of the Monastery of Yuste. *See* Monteiro (Mariana).
Monks of Iona and the Duke of Argyll. *See* M'Corry.
MONSABRE (Rev. Pere), Gold and Alloy. 12mo., 2s. 6d.
MONTAGU (Lord Robert), Civilization and the See of Rome. 8vo., 6d.
Montalembert (Count de). By George White. 12mo., 6d.
MONTEIRO (Mariana), Allah Akbar—God is Great. An Arab Legend of the Siege and Conquest of Granada. 12mo., 3s. 6d.
——— Monk of the Monastery of Yuste; or, The Last Days of the Emperor Charles V. An Historical Legend of the 16th Century. 12mo., 2s. 6d.
——— Gathered Gems from Spanish Authors. 12mo., 3s.
——— Sanctuary Meditations. *See* Gracian.
Mora (Ven. Elizabeth Canori), Life of. Translated from the Italian, with Preface by Lady Herbert. With Photograph, 12mo. 3s. 6d.
MULHOLLAND (Rosa), Prince and Saviour: The Story of Jesus. 12mo., Coloured Illustrations, 2s. 6d.; 32mo., 6d.
MULLER (Rev. M.), The Holy Mass. 12mo., 10s. 6d.
Multiplication Table, on a sheet. 3s. per 100.
MURRAY-LANE (Chevalier H.), Chronological Sketch of the Kings of England and the Kings of France. 12mo. 2s. 6d.; or in 2 vols., 1s. 6d. each.
MUSIC : Ave Maria, for Four Voices. By W. Schulthes. 1s. 3d.
    Cæcilian Society. *See* Separate List. Price 1s. or 2s.
    Catholic Choralist. Monthly, 3d.
    Catholic Hymnal (English Words). For one, two, or four voices, with accompaniment. By Leopold de Prins. 4to., 2s.; bound, 3s.
    Cor Jesu, Salus in Te sperantium. By W. Schulthes, 2s.; with Harp Accompaniment, 2s. 6d.; abridged, 3d.
    Corona Lauretana. 20 Litanies by W. Schulthes. 2s.
    Evening Hymn at the Oratory. By Rev. J. Nary. 3d.
    Litanies (36) and Benediction Service. By W. Schulthes. 6s. Second Series (Corona Lauretana). 2s.
    Litanies (6). By E. Leslie. 6d.
    Litanies (18). By Rev. J. McCarthy. 1s. 3d.
    Litany of the B.V.M. By Baronnesse Emma Freemantle. 6d. [Schaller. 2s. 6d.
    Mass of St. Patrick. For three equal voices. By F.

Mass of the Holy Child Jesus. In Unison. By W. Schulthes. 3s. The vocal part only, 4d.; or 3s. per doz. Cloth, 6d.; or 4s. 6d. per doz.

Ne projicias me a facie Tua. Motett for Four Voices. By W. Schulthes. 1s. 3d.

Oratory Hymns. By W. Schulthes. 2 vols., 8s.

Recordare. Oratorio Jeremiæ Prophetæ. By the same. 1s.

Regina Cœli. Motett for Four Voices. By W. Schulthes. 3s. Vocal Arrangement, 1s.

Six Sacred Vocal Pieces, for three or four equal Voices. By W. Schulthes. 4s.

Six Invocations, for four equal Voices. By W. Schulthes. 1s. 6d.

Twelve Latin Hymns. By W. Schulthes. 1s. 6d.

Veni Domine. Motett for Four Voices. By W. Schulthes. 2s. Vocal Arrangement, 6d.

Vespers and Benediction Service. Composed and harmonized by Leopold de Prins. 4to., 3s. 6d.

*** *All the above (music) prices are nett.*

My Conversion and Vocation. By Rev. Father Schouvaloff, 5s.

My Godmother's Stories from many Lands. By Mrs. T. K. Hervey. 12mo., 3s. 6d.

My Golden Days. By M. F. S. 12mo., 2s. 6d., or in 3 vols., 1s. each; or 1s. 6d. gilt.

NARY (Rev. J.) Evening Hymn at the Oratory. Music, 3d.

Necessity of Enquiry as to Religion. *See* Pye (Henry John).

NEVIN (Willis, Esq.), The Jesuits, and other Essays. 12mo., 1s.; cloth, 2s. 6d.

NEWMAN (Rev. Dr.), Miscellanies, 6s.; Critical and Historical Essays, 2 vols., 12s.; Tracts, Theological and Ecclesiastical, 8s.; Certain Difficulties felt by Anglicans, second series, 5s. 6d. Via Media, 2 vols., 12s. Development, 6s.

—— Characteristics from the Writings of. By W. S. Lilly. 12mo., 6s.

New Testament. 12mo., 2s. 6d. Persian calf, 7s. 6d., morocco, 10s. Illustrated, large 4to., 7s. 6d.

New Year's Gift to Our Heavenly Father. 32mo., 4d.

Nicholas; or, the Reward of a Good Action. 18mo., 6d.

NICHOLS (T. L.), Forty Years of American Life. 5s.

Nina and Pippo, the Lost Children of Mt. St. Bernard. 6d.

NOETHEN'S (Rev. T.), Good Thoughts for Priests and People; or, Short Meditations for every Day in the Year. 8s.

—— Compendium of the History of the Catholic Church. 12mo., 8s.

—— History of the Catholic Church. 12mo., 5s. 6d.

Novena to Our Blessed Lady of Lourdes for the use of the Sick. 18mo., 4d.

Novena of Grace, revealed by S. Francis Xavier. 18mo., 6d.

Novena of Meditations in honour of St. Joseph, according to the method of St. Ignatius, preceded by a new method of hearing Mass according to the intentions of the Souls in Purgatory. 18mo., 1s.

R. Washbourne, 18 Paternoster Row, London.

Occasional Prayers for Festivals. *See* Prayers, page 31.
O'CLERY (Keyes, M.P., K.S.G.), The History of the Italian Revolution. First Period—The Revolution of the Barricades (1796-1849). 8vo., 7s. 6d. Cheap edition 3s. 6d.
O'Connell the Liberator. *See* Cusack (M. F.).
O'GALLAGHER (Dr.), Sermons in Irish-Gælic; with literal idiomatic English Translation, and a Memoir of the Bishop, by Canon U. J. Bourke. 8vo., 7s. 6d.
O'Hagan (Mary), Life of. By Miss Cusack. 8vo., 6s.
O'HAIRE (Rev. J.), Recollections of South Africa. 7s. 6d.
O'MAHONY (D.P.M.), Rome semper eadem. 8vo., 1s. 6d.
O'MEARA (Kathleen), The Battle of Connemara. 12mo., 3s.
———— *See* Grace Ramsay.
On what Authority do I accept Christianity? 12mo., 6d.
Oratorian Lives of the Saints. With Portrait, 12mo., 5s. a vol.
   I. S. Bernardine of Siena, Minor Observatine.
   II. S. Philip Benizi, Fifth General of the Servites.
   III. S. Veronica Giuliani, and B. Battista Varani.
   IV. S. John of God. By Canon Cianfogni.
O'REILLY (Rev. Dr.), Victims of the Mamertine. 5s.
————A Romance of Repentance. 12mo., 3s. 6d.
Oremus, A Liturgical Prayer Book. *See* p. 31.
Our Lady's Comfort to the Sorrowful. 32mo., 6d. and 1s.
Our Lady (Devotion to) in North America. *See* Macleod.
Our Lady's Lament. *See* Tame (C.E.).
Our Lady's Month. By Rev. A. P. Bethell. 18mo., 1s. 6d.
Our Legends and Lives. By E. L. Hervey. 12mo., 6s.
Our Lord's Life, Passion, Death, and Resurrection. Translated from Ribadeneira. 12mo., 1s.
———— By Rev. H. Rutter. Illustrated. 12mo., 5s.
———— Incidents. A Series of 12 Illuminations. 4to., 6s.
OXENHAM (H. N.), Dr. Pusey's Eirenicon. 8vo., 6d.
———— Poems. 12mo., 3s. 6d.
Oxford Undergraduate of Twenty Years Ago. By a Bachelor of Arts. 8vo., 2s. 6d.; cloth, 3s. 6d.
OZANAM (A. F.), Protestantism and Liberty. Translated from the French by Wilfrid C. Robinson. 8vo., 1s.
Pale (The) and the Septs. A Romance of the XVI. Century. 6s.
Panegyrics of Fr. Segneri, S.J. Translated from the original Italian. With a Preface, by Rev. W. Humphrey, S.J. 12mo., 5s.
Paradise of God; or the Virtues of the Sacred Heart. By Author of "God our Father," "Happiness of Heaven." 12mo., 4s.
Paray le Monial, and Bl. Margaret Mary. 18mo., 6d.
Passion of Our Lord, Harmony of. *See* Gayrard (Mme.).
PASSIONIST FATHERS: Mirror of Faith. 12mo., 3s.
    Manual of the Cross and Passion. 32mo., 3s.
    Sacred Eloquence. 18mo., 2s.
    S. Paul of the Cross. 12mo., 3s.
    School of Jesus Crucified. 18mo., 5s.
Pastor and People. By Rev. T. J. Potter. 12mo., 5s.
Path to Paradise. *See* Prayers, page 31.
Patrick (S.), Life of. 1s.; 8vo., 6s.; gilt, 10s.; 4to., 20s.

Patrick's (S.) Manual. By Miss Cusack. 18mo., 3s. 6d.
Patron Saints. By E. A. Starr. Illustrated. 12mo., 10s.
Pearl among the Virtues. By Rev. P. A. De Doss. 12mo., 3s.
Penitential Psalms. See Blyth (Rev. F.).
PENS, Washbourne's Free and Easy. Fine, or Middle, or Broad Points, 1s. per gross.
Percy Grange. By Rev. T. J. Potter. 12mo., 3s.
Perpetual Adoration, Book of. Boudon. 12mo., 3s. and 3s. 6d.
Peter (S.), his Name and his Office. See Allies (T. W., Esq.).
Peter, Years of. By an ex-Papal Zouave. 12mo., 1d.
Philip Benizi (S.), Life of. See Oratorian Lives of the Saints.
Philomena (S.), Life and Miracles of. 12mo., 2s. 6d.
Philosophy, Elements of. By Rev. W. H. Hill. 8vo., 6s.
PHILPIN (Rev. F.), Holy Places; their sanctity and authenticity. With three Maps. 12mo., 2s. 6d. and 6s.
Photographs (10) illustrating the History of the Miraculous Hosts, called the Blessed Sacrament of the Miracle. 2s. 6d. the set.
Pius IX. 32mo., 6d.; 4to., 1d.
Pius IX., from his Birth to his Death. By G. White. 12mo., 6d.
Pius IX., his early Life to the Return from Gaeta. By Rev. T. B. Snow, O.S.B. 12mo., 6d.
Plain Chant. See Gregorian.
———— The Cecilian Society Music kept in stock.
PLATUS (Rev. F.), Origin and Progress of Religious Orders, and Happiness of a Religious State. 12mo., 2s. 6d.
PLAYS. See Dramas, page 10.
POIRIER (Bishop), A General Catechism of the Christian Doctrine. 18mo., 9d.
POOR CLARES OF KENMARE. See Cusack (Miss).
Pope-King, Rule of. By Rev. E. R. Martin. 8vo., 6d.
Pope of Rome. See Tondini (Rev. C.).
Popes, Lives of the Early. See Meyrick (Rev. T.).
POTTER (Rev. T. J.), Extempory Preaching. 5s.
———— Farleyes of Farleye. 12mo., 2s. 6d.
———— Pastor and People. 12mo., 5s.
———— Percy Grange. 12mo., 3s.
———— Rupert Aubrey. 12mo., 3s.
———— Sir Humphrey's Trial. 16mo., 2s. 6d.
POWELL (J., Esq.), Two Years in the Pontifical Zouaves. Illustrated. 8vo., 3s. 6d.
POWER (Rev. P.) Catechism. 3 vols., 10s. 6d.; 2 vols. 7s. 6d.
PRADEL (Fr., O. P.), Life of St. Vincent Ferrer. Translated by Rev. Fr. Dixon. With a Photograph. 12mo., 5s.
PRAYER BOOKS. See page 30.
PRINS (Leopold de). See Music.
Pro-Cathedral, Kensington. Tinted View of the Interior, 11 × 15 inches, 1s.; Proofs, on larger paper, 2s.
Prophecies, Contemporary. By Mgr. Dupanloup. 8vo., 1s.
Protestantism and Liberty. See Robinson (W. C.).
Protestant Principles examined by the Written Word. 1s.

Prussian Spy. A Novel. By V. Valmont. 12mo., 4s.
Purgatory, A Novena in favour of the Souls in. 32mo., 3d.
Purgatory, Month of the Souls in Purgatory. By Ricard, 1s.
Purgatory, The Doctrine of. By Rev. W. Marshall. 12mo., 1s.
Purgatory, Souls in. By Abbot Burder. 32mo., 3d.
Pusey's (Dr.) Eirenicon considered. *See* Oxenham (H. N.).
PYE (Henry John, M.A.), Necessity of Enquiry as to Religion. 32mo., 4d.; cloth, 6d.
——— The Religion of Common Sense. New Edition. 1s.
——— Are the Ritualists Catholic? 8vo., 6d.
RAMIERE (Rev. H.), Apostleship of Prayer. 12mo., 6s.
RAVIGNAN (Pere), The Spiritual Life, Conferences. Translated by Mrs. Abel Ram. 12mo., 5s.
Ravignan (Pere), Life of. 12mo., 9s.
RAWES (Rev. F.), Homeward. 2s. Sursum. 1s.
Reading Lessons. By the Marist Brothers. 12mo., 1st Book, 4d.; 2nd Book, 7d.
REDMAN (Rev. Dr.), Book of Perpetual Adoration. By Mgr. Boudon. 12mo., 3s.; red edges, 3s. 6d. [18mo., 1s.
REDMOND (Rev. Dr.), Eight Short Sermon Essays.
REEVE'S History of the Bible. 12mo., 3s. 6d. 18mo., 1s.
Reflections, One Hundred Pious. *See* Butler.
Regina Sæculorum; or, Mary Venerated in all Ages. Devotions to the Blessed Virgin from Ancient Sources. 12mo., 1s. and 3s.
Rejection of Catholic Doctrines attributable to the Non-Realization of Primary Truths. 8vo., 1s.
Religion of Common Sense. By H. J. Pye, M.A. 12mo., 1s.
Religious Orders. *See* Platus (Rev. F.).
Rest, on the Cross. By Eleanora Louisa Hervey. 12mo., 3s. 6d.
Reverse of the Medal. A Drama for Girls. 12mo., 6d.
RIBADENEIRA—Life, Passion, Death, and Resurrection of our Lord. 12mo., 1s.
RICARD (Abbe), Month of the Holy Angels. 18mo., 1s.
——— Month of the Souls in Purgatory. 18mo., 1s.
RICHARDSON (Rev. Fr.), Catholic Sick and Benefit Club; or, the Guild of our Lady; and St. Joseph's Catholic Burial Society. 32mo., 4d.
——— Little by Little; or, the Penny Bank. 32mo., 1d.
——— Shamrocks. 6s. 2d. a gross (144), post free.
——— S. Joseph's Catholic Burial Society. 2d.
——— The Crusade; or, Catholic Association for the Suppression of Drunkenness. 32mo., 1d.
Ritus Servandus in Expositione et Benedictione S.S. 4to., cloth, 5s. 6d.
Road to Heaven. A Game. By Miss M. A. Macdaniel. 3s. 6d.
ROBERTSON (Professor), Lectures on the Life, Writings, and Times of Edmund Burke. 12mo., 3s. 6d.
——— Lectures on Modern History and Biography. 6s.
ROBINSON (Wilfrid C.), Protestantism and Liberty. Translated from the French of Professor Ozanam. 8vo., 1s.
Roman Question, The. By Rev. Dr. Husenbeth. 8vo., 6d.
Rome and her Captors: Letters collected and edited by Count Henri d'Ideville, and Translated by F. R. Wegg-Prosser. 4s.

Rome, Past, Present, and Future. By Dr. M'Corry. 8vo., 6d.
——— Personal Recollections of. By W. J. Jacob, 8vo., 6d.
——— The Victories of. By Rev. F. Beste. 8vo., 1s.
——— (To) and Back. Fly-Leaves from a Flying Tour. Edited by Rev. W. H. Anderdon, S.J., 12mo., 2s.
Rosalie; or, the Memoir of a French Child, told by herself. 12mo., 1s.; stronger bound, 1s. 6d.; gilt, 2s.
Rosary, Fifteen Mysteries of, and Fourteen Stations of the Cross. In One Volume, 32 Illustrations. 16mo., 2s.
Rosary for the Souls in Purgatory, with Indulgenced Prayer. 6d. and 9d. Medals separately, 1d. each, or 9s. gross. Prayers separately, 1d. each, 9d. a dozen, or 6s. for 100.
Rosary, Chats about the. *See* Aunt Margaret's Little Neighbours.
ROWLEY (Rev. Austin John), A Devout Exposition of the Holy Mass. Composed by John Heigham. 12mo., 4s.
RUSSELL (Rev. M.) Eucharistic Verses. 12mo., 2s.
RUTTER (Rev. H.) Life and Sufferings of Our Lord, with Introduction by Rev. Dr. Husenbeth. Illustrated. 12mo., 5s.
RYAN (Bishop). What Catholics do not Believe. 12mo., 1s.
Sacred Heart, Act of Consecration to. 1d.; or 6s. per 100.
——————————, Act of Reparation to. 1s. 2d. per 100.
——————————, A Spiritual Banquet. 6d.
——————————, Devotions to. By Rev. S. Franco. 12mo., 4s.; cheap edition, 2s. [cloth, 6d.; gilt, 1s.
——————————, Devotions to. By Bishop Milner. 32mo., 3d.;
——————————, Devotions to. Translated by Rev. J. Joy Dean. 12mo., 2s. [12mo., 3s.
——————————, Elevations to the. By Rev. Fr. Doyotte, S.J.
——————————, Handbook of the Confraternity, for the use of Members. 18mo., 3d.
——————————, Little Treasury of. 32mo., 2s.; French morocco, 2s. 6d.; calf, 5s.; morocco, 6s.
——————————, Manual of Devotions to the, from the writings of Blessed Margaret Mary. 32mo., 3d.
—————————— offered to the Piety of the Young engaged in Study. By Rev. F. Deham. 32mo., 6d.
—————————— *See* Paradise of God; Kinane (Rev. T. H.).
——————————, Pleadings of. By Rev. M. Comerford. 18mo., 1s.; gilt edges, 2s.; with Handbook of the Confraternity, 1s. 6d.
——————————, Treasury of. 18mo., 3s. 6d.; roan, 4s.
Sacred History in Forty Pictures. Plain, 5s.; coloured, 7s. 6d.; mounted on cardboard, coloured, 18s. 6d. and 22s.
Saints, Lives of. By Alban Butler. 4 vols., 8vo., 32s.; gilt, 50s.; and leather, gilt, 64s.; or the 4 vols. in 2, 28s.; gilt, 34s.
——————————. for every day in the Year. Beautifully printed, within illustrated borders from ancient sources, on thick toned paper. 4to., gilt, 21s.
——— Patron. By E. A. Starr. Illustrated. 12mo., 10s.
ST. JURE (S.J.) Knowledge and Love of Jesus Christ. 3 vols., 8vo., 30s.
——— The Spiritual Man. 12mo., 6s.

R. Washbourne, 18 Paternoster Row, London.

Sanctuary Meditations for Priests and Frequent Communicants. Translated from the Spanish of Fr. Baltasar Gracian, by Mariana Monteiro. 12mo., 4s.

SCARAMELLI—**Directorium Asceticum**; or, Guide to the Spiritual Life. 4 vols. 12mo., 24s. Vols. 4, 3, or 2 sold separately, 6s. each.

SCHMID (Canon), Tales. Illustrated. 12mo., 3s. 6d. Separately:—The Canary Bird, The Dove, The Inundation, The Rose Tree, The Water Jug, The Wooden Cross. 6d. each; gilt, 1s.

SCHOOL BOOKS. Supplied according to order.

School of Jesus Crucified. By the Passionist Fathers. 18mo., 5s.

SCHOUVALOFF (Rev. Father, Barnabite), My Conversion and Vocation. Translated from the French, with an Appendix, by Fr. C. Tondini. 12mo., 5s.

SCHULTHES (William). See Music.

Scraps from my Scrapbook. See Arnold (M. J.).

SEGNERI (Fr., S.J.), Panegyrics. Translated from the original Italian. With a Preface, by Rev. W. Humphrey. 12mo., 5s.

SEGUR (Mgr.), Books for Little Children. Translated. 32mo., 3d. each. Confession, Holy Communion, Child Jesus, Piety, Prayer, Temptation and Sin. In one volume, cloth, 2s.

—————— **Practical Counsels for Holy Communion.** 18mo., 1s.

SEGUR (Countess de), The Little Hunchback. 12mo., 3s.

Seigneret (Paul), Life of. 12mo., 6d., 1s., and 1s. 6d.; gilt, 2s.

Selea; a Collection of Matter for Sermons. By St. Liguori. 12mo., 5s.

Semi-Tropical Trifles. By H. Compton. 12mo., 1s.; cloth, 2s. 6d.

Sermon Essays. By Rev. Dr. Redmond. 12mo., 1s.

Sermons. Irish and English. By Dr. O'Gallagher. 8vo., 7s. 6d.

—————— By Father Burke, O.P., and others. 12mo., 2s.

—————— The Light of the Holy Spirit in the World. By Bishop Hedley. 1s.; cloth, 1s. 6d.

—————— One Hundred Short. By Rev. Fr. Thomas. 8vo., 12s.

Sermons, Lectures, &c. By Rev. M. M. Buckley. 12mo., 6s.

Serving Boy's Manual, and Book of Public Devotions. Containing all those prayers and devotions for Sundays and Holydays, usually divided in their recitation between the Priest and the Congregation. Compiled from approved sources, and adapted to Churches, served either by the Secular or Regular Clergy. 32mo., embossed, 1s.; French morocco, 2s.; calf, 4s.; with Epistles and Gospels, 6d. extra.

Seven Sacraments Explained and Defended. 18mo., 1s. 6d.

SHAKESPEARE. Expurgated edition. By Rosa Baughan. 8vo., 6s. The Comedies only, 3s. 6d.

Shandy Maguire. A Farce for Boys. 2 Acts. 12mo., 2s.

SHAW (T. H.), Holy Church the Centre of Unity; or, Ritualism compared with Catholicism. 8vo., 1s.

Siege of Limerick (Florence O'Neill). See Stewart (Agnes M.).

SIGHART (Dr.) Albertus Magnus. 10s. 6d. Cheap edition, 5s.

Silver Teapot. By Elizabeth King. 18mo., 4d.

Simple Tales—Waiting for Father, &c., &c. 16mo., 2s. 6d.

Sir Ælfric and other Tales. *See* Bampfield (Rev. G.).
Sir Humphrey's Trial. By Rev. T. J. Potter. 16mo., 2s. 6d.
Sir Thomas Maxwell and his Ward. By Miss Bridges. 12mo, 1s. and 2s.
Sisters of Charity, Manual of. 18mo. 6s.
SMITH-SLIGO (A. V., Esq.), Life of the Ven. Anna Maria Taigi. Translated from French of Calixte. 8vo., 2s. 6d. and 5s.
— (Mrs.) Margarethe Verflassen. 12mo., 1s. 6d., 3s., and 3s. 6d.
SNOW (Rev. T. B.), Pius IX., His early Life to the Return from Gaeta. 12mo., 6d.
Soul (The), United to Jesus. 32mo., 1s. 6d.
SPALDING'S (Abp.) Works. 5 vols., 52s. 6d.; or separately: Evidences of Catholicity, 10s. 6d.; Miscellanea, 2 vols., 21s.; Protestant Reformation, 2 vols., 21s.; cheap edition, 1 vol., 14s.
Spalding (Archbishop), Life of. 8vo., 10s. 6d.
——— Sermon at the Month's Mind. 8vo., 1s.
Spiritual Conferences on the Mysteries of Faith and the Interior Life. By Father Collins. 12mo., 5s.
Spiritual Life. Conferences by Père Ravignan. Translated by Mrs. Abel Ram. 12mo., 5s.
Spiritual Works of Louis of Blois. Edited by Rev. F. John Bowden. 12mo., 3s. 6d.; red edges, 4s.
Spouse of Christ. By Sister M. F. Clare. 12mo., vol. 2, 7s. 6d.
STARR (Eliza Allen), Patron Saints. Illustrated. 12mo., 10s.
Stations of the Cross, Devotions for Public and Private Use at the. By Miss Cusack. Illustrated. 16mo., 1s. and 1s. 6d.
Stations of the Cross. By S. Liguori. 18mo., 1d.
Stations of the Cross and Mysteries of the Rosary. 2s.
STEWART (A. M.), Alone in the World. 12mo., 4s. 6d.
——— St. Angela's Manual. *See* Angela (S.).
——— Biographical Readings. 12mo., 4s. 6d.
——— Cardinal Wolsey. 12mo., 6s. 6d.
——— Sir Thomas More. Illustrated, 10s. 6d.; gilt, 11s. 6d.
——— Life of S. Angela Merici. 12mo., 4s. 6d.
——— Life in the Cloister. 12mo., 3s. 6d. [extra, 6s.
——— Limerick Veteran; or, the Foster Sisters. 12mo., 5s.;
——— Margaret Roper. 12mo., 6s.; extra, 7s. [16mo., 1s.
Stories for my Children—The Angels and the Sacraments.
Stories of Holy Lives. By M. F. S. 12mo., 3s. 6d.
Stories of Martyr Priests. By M. F. S. 12mo., 3s. 6d.
Stories of the Saints. By M. F. S. 12mo., 1st Series, 3s. 6d.; gilt, 4s. 6d. 2nd Series, 3s. 6d.; gilt, 4s. 6d. 3rd Series, 3s. 6d.
Stormsworth, with other Poems and Plays. By the author of "Thy Gods, O Israel.' 12mo., 3s. 6d.
Story of an Orange Lodge. 12mo., 1s.
Story of Marie and other Tales. 12mo., 2s.; gilt, 3s., or separately:—The Story of Marie, 2d.; Nelly Blane, and a Contrast, 2d.; A Conversion and a Death-bed, 2d.; Herbert Montagu, 2d.; Jane Murphy, the Dying Gipsy, and the Nameless Grave, 2d.; The Beggars, and True and False Riches, 2d.; Pat and his Friend, 2d.

R. Washbourne, 18 *Paternoster Row, London.*

Story of the Life of St. Paul. By M. F. S., author of "Stories of the Saints." 12mo., 2s. 6d.

Sufferings of our Lord. Sermons preached by Father Claude de la Colombière, S.J., in the Chapel Royal, St. James's, in the year 1677. 18mo., 1s.; stronger bound, 1s. 6d.; red edges, 2s.

Supernatural Life, The. By Mgr. Mermillod. Translated from the French, with a Preface by Lady Herbert. 12mo., 5s.

Supremacy of the Roman See. By C. E. Tame, Esq. 8vo., 6d.

Sure Way to Heaven. A Little Manual for Confession and Holy Communion. 32mo., 6d.; Persian, 2s. 6d.; calf or morocco, 3s. 6d.

Sweetness of Holy Living; or, Honey culled from the Flower Garden of S. Francis of Sales. 18mo., 1s.; French morocco, 3s.

Taigi (Anna Maria), Life of. Translated from the French of Calixte by A. V. Smith-Sligo, Esq. 8vo., 2s. 6d. and 5s.

Tales and Sketches. *See* Fleet (Charles).

Tales of the Jewish Church. By Charles Walker. 12mo., 2s. 6d.

TAME (C. E., Esq.), Early English Literature. 16mo., 2s. a vol. I. Our Lady's Lament, and the Lamentation of S. Mary Magdalene. II. Life of Our Lady, in verse.

―――― **Supremacy of the Roman See.** 8vo., 6d.

TANDY (Rev. Dr.), Terry O'Flinn. 12mo., 1s.; stronger bound, 1s. 6d.; gilt, 2s.

TAUNTON (M.), Last of the Catholic O'Malleys. 18mo., 1s. 6d.; stronger bound, 2s.

―――― **One Hundred Pious Reflections,** from Alban Butler's Lives of the Saints. 18mo., 1s.; stronger bound, 2s.

Temperance Books. *See* Richardson (Rev. Fr.).

―――― Cards (Illuminated), 3d. each. [3d. each.

―――― Medals—Immaculate Conception, St. Patrick, St. Joseph.

Terry O'Flinn. By Rev. Dr. Tandy. 12mo., 1s., 1s. 6d. and 2s.

Testimony; or, the Necessity of Enquiry as to Religion. By John Henry Pye, M.A. 32mo., 4d.; cloth, 6d.

THOMAS (H. J.), One Hundred Short Sermons. 8vo., 12s.

Three Wishes. A Tale. By M. F. S. 12mo., 2s. 6d.

Threshold of the Catholic Church. *See* Bagshawe (Rev. J. B.)

Tim O'Halloran's Choice. *See* Cusack.

Tom's Crucifix, and other Tales. By M. F. S. 12mo., 3s., or in 5 vols., 1s. each; gilt, 1s. 6d.

TONDINI (Rev. Cæsarius), My Conversion and Vocation. By Rev. Fr. Schouvaloff. 12mo., 5s.

―――― **The Pope of Rome and the Popes of the Oriental Orthodox Church.** An essay on Monarchy in the Church, with special reference to Russia. Second Edition. 12mo., 3s. 6d.

―――― **Some Documents concerning of the Association Prayers in Honour of Mary Immaculate, for the Return of the Greek-Russian Church to Catholic Unity.** 12mo., 3d. Association of Prayers, 32mo., 1d.

Transubstantiation, Catholic Doctrine of. 12mo., 6d.

Trials of Faith. *See* Browne (E. G. K.).

TRONSON (Abbe), The Mass: a devout Method. 32mo., 4d.

TRONSON'S Conferences for Ecclesiastical Students and Religious. By Sister M. F. Clare. 12mo., 4s. 6d.
Two Colonels. By Father Thomas. 12mo., 6s. [gilt, 1s. 6d.
Two Friends; or Marie's Self-Denial. By Madame d'Arras. 1s., or
Ursuline Manual. *See* Prayers, page 32.
VALMONT (V.), The Prussian Spy. A Novel. 12mo., 4s.
VAUGHAN (Bishop of Salford), Holy Sacrifice of the Mass. 2d.; cloth, 6d.
——— **Love and Passion of Jesus Christ.** 2d.
VERE (Rev. G. L.), The Catholic Hymn Book. 32mo., 2d.; cloth, 4d. Appendix containing Hymns in honour of Saints. 1d.
Veronica Giuliani (S.), Life of, and B. Battista Varani. With a Photographic Portrait. 12mo., 5s.
Village Lily. A Tale. 12mo., 1s.; gilt, 1s. 6d.
Vincent Ferrer (S.), of the Order of Friar Preachers; his Life, Spiritual Teaching, and Practical Devotion. By Rev. Fr. Andrew Pradel, O.P. Translated from the French by the Rev. Fr. T. A. Dixon, O.P., with a Photograph. 12mo., 5s.
VINCENT OF LIRINS (S.). Commonitory. 12mo., 1s. 3d.
Vincent of Paul (S.), Glory of. *See* Manning (Archbishop).
VIRGIL. Literally translated by Davidson. 12mo., 2s. 6d.
"Vitis Mystica"; or, the True Vine. *See* Brownlow.
WALKER (Charles), Are You Safe in the Church of England? 8vo., 6d.
——— **Tales of the Jewish Church.** 12mo., 2s. 6d.
WALLER (J. F., Esq.), Festival Tales. 12mo., 3s. 6d.
Way of Salvation. By S. Liguori. 32mo., 1s.
WEBB (Alfred), Compendium of Irish Biography. 8vo., 16s.
Weedall (Mgr.), Life of. By Rev. Dr. Husenbeth. 8vo., 1s.
WEGG-PROSSER (F. R.), Rome and her Captors. 4s.
Wenefred (St.), Life of. By Rev. T. Meyrick. 12mo., 2s.
What Catholics do not Believe. By Bishop Ryan. 12mo., 1s.
WENINGER (Rev. F. X., S.J.), Lives of the Saints for every day in the Year. Illustrated. 4to., 2 vols., or 12 vols., 50s.
WHITE (George), Cardinal Wiseman. 12mo., 1s. and 1s. 6d.
——— **Comte de Montalembert.** 12mo., 6d.
——— **Life of S. Edmund of Canterbury.** 1s. and 1s. 6d.
——— **Pius IX., from his Birth to his Death.** 12mo., 6d.
William (St.), of York. A Drama in Two Acts. (Boys.) 12mo., 6d.
WILLIAMS (Canon), Anglican Orders. 12mo., 3s. 6d.
Wiseman (Cardinal), Life and Obsequies. 1s. and 1s. 6d.
——— **Recollections of.** By M. J. Arnold. 12mo., 2s. 6d.
WOODS (Canon), Defence of the Roman Church against F. Gratry. Translated from the French of Gueranger. 1s. 6d.
WYATT-EDGELL (Alfred), Stormsworth, with other Poems and Plays. 12mo., 3s. 6d.
——— **Thy Gods! O Israel.** 12mo., 2s.
Young Catholic's Guide to Confession and Holy Communion. By Dr. Kenny. 32mo., 4d.; cloth, 6d.; red edges, 9d., French morocco, 1s. 6d.; calf or morocco, 2s. 6d.
YOUNG (T., Esq.), History of Ireland. 18mo., 2s. 6d.
Zouaves, Pontifical, Two Years in. By Joseph Powell, Z.P. Illustrated. 8vo., 3s. 6d.

Garden, Little, of the Soul. Edited by the Rev. R. G. Davis. *With Imprimatur of the Archbishop of Westminster.* This book, as its name imports, contains a selection from the "Garden of the Soul" of the Prayers and Devotions of most general use. Whilst it will serve as a *Pocket Prayer Book* for all, it is, by its low price, *par excellence*, the Prayer Book for children and for the very poor. In it are to be found the old familiar Devotions of the "Garden of the Soul," as well as many important additions, such as the Devotions to the Sacred Heart, to Saint Joseph, to the Guardian Angels, and others. The omissions are mainly the Forms of administering the Sacraments, and Devotions that are not of very general use. It is printed in a clear type, on a good paper, both especially selected, for the purpose of obviating the disagreeableness of small type and inferior paper. Twentieth Thousand.

32mo., price, cloth, 6d.; with rims, 1s. Embossed, red edges, 9d.; with rims and clasp, 1s. 3d.; Strong roan, 1s.; with rims and clasp, 1s. 6d. French morocco, 1s. 6d.; with rims and clasp, 2s. French morocco extra gilt, 2s.; with rims and clasp, 2s. 6d. Calf or morocco, 3s.; with rims and clasp, 4s. Calf or morocco, extra gilt, 4s.; with rims and clasp, 5s. Morocco antique, 7s. 6d., 10s. 6d., 12s., 16s. Velvet, rims and clasp, 5s., 8s. 6d., and 10s. 6d. Russia, 5s.; with clasp, &c., 8s.; Russia antique, 17s. 6d. Ivory, with rims and clasp, 10s. 6d., 13s., 15s., 17s. 6d. Imitation ivory, with rims and clasp, 3s. With oxydized silver or gilt mountings, in morocco case, 25s.

Cheap edition with Epistles and Gospels, 6d., or better bound with clasp, 1s.

Catholic Hours: a Manual of Prayer, including Mass and Vespers. By J. R. Digby Beste, Esq. 32mo., cloth, 2s.; red edges, 2s. 6d.; roan, 3s.; morocco, 6s.

Catholic Piety; or, Key of Heaven, with Epistles and Gospels. Large 32mo., roan, 1s. 6d. and 2s.; French morocco, with rims and clasp, 2s. 6d.; extra gilt, 3s.; with rims and clasp, 3s. 6d.

Catholic Piety; or, Key of Heaven. 32mo., 6d.; rims and clasp, 1s.; French morocco, 1s.; velvet, with rims and clasp, 2s. 6d.; with Epistles and Gospels, roan, 1s.; French morocco, 1s. 6d.; with rims and clasp, 2s.; extra gilt, 2s.; Persian, 2s. 6d.; imitation ivory, 3s.; morocco, 3s. 6d.; velvet, rims and clasp, 3s. 6d.

Crown of Jesus. 18mo., Persian calf, 6s. Calf or Morocco, 7s. 6d. and 8s. 6d.; with rims and clasp, 10s. 6d. Calf or morocco, extra gilt, 10s. 6d.; with rims and clasp, 12s. 6d; with turn-over edges, 10s. 6d. Ivory, with rims and clasp, 21s., 25s., 27s. 6d. and 30s.

Daily Exercises for Devout Christians. By Rev. P. V. Monk, O.S.B. 18mo., 3s. 6d.

Devotions for Mass. Very large type, 12mo., 2d.

Garden of the Soul. Very large Type. 18mo., cloth, 1s.; with Epistles and Gospels, 1s. 6d.; French morocco, 2s. 6d.; with E. and G., 3s. 6d. Best edition, without E. and G., 3s. 6d.; with E. and G., morocco circuit, 7s. 6d.; calf antique, with clasp, 8s.; French morocco, antique, with clasp, 6s. 6d.

Epistles and Gospels, in French morocco, 2s.

Holy Childhood. Simple Prayers for very little children. 32mo., 1s.; gilt, 1s. 6d.; cheap edition, 6d.
Illustrated Manual of Prayers. 32mo., 3d.; cloth, 4d.
Key of Heaven. *Very large type.* 18mo., 1s.; leather, 2s. 6d.
Lily of St. Joseph, The; a little Manual of Prayers and Hymns for Mass. 64mo., price 2d.; cloth, 3d., 4d., 6d., or 8d.; roan, 1s.; French morocco, 1s. 6d.; calf or morocco, 2s.; gilt, 2s. 6d.
Little Prayer Book, The, for Ordinary Catholic Devotions. 3d.
Manual of Catholic Devotions. Small, for the waistcoat pocket. 64mo., 4d.; with Epistles and Gospels, cloth, 6d.; with rims, 1s.; roan, 1s.; with tuck, 1s. 6d.; calf or morocco, 2s. 6d.; ivorine, 2s. 6d.
Manual of Devotions in Honour of our Lady of Sorrows. 18mo., 1s. 6d.; cheaper binding, 1s.
Manual of the Sisters of Charity. 18mo., 6s.
Memorare Mass. By Sister M. F. Clare, of Kenmare 32mo., 2d.
Missal (Complete). 18mo., Persian, 8s. 6d.; calf or morocco, 10s. 6d.; with rims and clasp, 13s. 6d.; calf or mor., extra gilt, 12s. 6d., with rims and clasp, 15s. 6d.; morocco, with turn-over edges, 13s. 6d.; morocco antique, 15s.; velvet, 20s.; Russia, 20s.; ivory, with rims and clasp, 31s. 6d. and 35s.
—— A very beautiful edition, handsomely bound in morocco, gilt mountings, silk linings, edges red on gold, in a morocco case. Illustrated, £5. [clasp, 8s.
Missal and Vesper Book, in one vol. 32mo., morocco, 6s.; with
Occasional Prayers for Festivals. 4d. and 6d.; gilt, 1s.
OREMUS, A Liturgical Prayer Book: with the Imprimatur of the Cardinal Archbishop of Westminster. An adaptation of the Church Offices: containing Morning and Evening Devotions; Devotion for Mass, Confession, and Communion, and various other Devotions; Common and Proper, Hymns, Lessons, Collects, Epistles and Gospels for Sundays, Feasts, and Week Days; and short notices of over 200 Saints' Days. 32mo., 452 pages, 2s.; cloth, 2s. 6d.; embossed, red edges, 3s. 6d.; French morocco, 4s. 6d.; calf, 5s. 6d.; morocco, 6s.; Russia, 8s. 6d., &c., &c., &c.
Path to Paradise. 32 full-page Illustrations. 32mo., cloth, 3d. With 50 Illustrations, cloth, 4d. Superior edition, 6d. and 1s.
Serving Boy's Manual and Book of Catholic Devotions, containing all those Prayers and Devotions for Sundays and Holidays, usually divided in their recitation between the Priest and the Congregation. Compiled from approved sources, and adapted to Churches served either by the Secular or the Regular Clergy, 32mo., Embossed, 1s.; with Epistles and Gospels, 1s. 6d.; French morocco, 2s., with Epistles and Gospels, 2s. 6d.; calf, 4s., with Epistles and Gospels, 4s. 6d.
Soul united to Jesus in the Adorable Sacrament. 1s. 6d.
S. Patrick's Manual. Compiled by Sister Mary Frances Clare. 3s. 6d.
Sure Way to Heaven. Cloth, 6d.: Persian, 2s. 6d.; morocco, 3s. 6d.
Treasury of the Sacred Heart. 18mo., 3s. 6d.; roan, 4s. 6d. 32mo., 2s.; French morocco, 2s. 6d.; calf 5s.; morocco, 6s.
Ursuline Manual. 18mo., 4s.; Persian calf, 7s. 6d.; morocco, 10s.

Garden of the Soul. (WASHBOURNE'S EDITION.) Edited by the Rev. R. G. Davis. *With Imprimatur of the Archbishop of Westminster.* Twenty-third Thousand. This Edition retains all the Devotions that have made the GARDEN OF THE SOUL, now for many generations, the well-known Prayer-book for English Catholics. During many years various Devotions have been introduced, and, in the form of appendices, have been added to other editions. These have now been incorporated into the body of the work, and, together with the Devotions to the Sacred Heart, to Saint Joseph, to the Guardian Angels, the Itinerarium, and other important additions, render this edition pre-eminently the Manual of Prayer, for both public and private use. The version of the Psalms has been carefully revised, and strictly conformed to the Douay translation of the Bible, published with the approbation of the LATE CARDINAL WISEMAN. The Forms of administering the Sacraments have been carefully translated, *as also the rubrical directions*, from the Ordo Administrandi Sacramenta. To enable all present, either at baptisms or other public administrations of the Sacraments, to pay due attention to the sacred rites, the Forms are inserted without any curtailment, both in Latin and English. The Devotions at Mass have been carefully revised, and enriched by copious adaptations from the prayers of the Missal. The preparation for the Sacraments of Penance and the Holy Eucharist have been the objects of especial care, to adapt them to the wants of those whose religious instruction may be deficient. Great attention has been paid to the quality of the paper and to the size of type used in the printing, to obviate that weariness so distressing to the eyes, caused by the use of books printed in small close type and on inferior paper.

32mo. Embossed, 1s.; with rims and clasp, 1s. 6d.; with Epistles and Gospels, 1s. 6d.; with rims and clasp, 2s. French morocco, 2s.; with rims and clasp, 2s. 6d.; with E. and G., 2s. 6d.; with rims and clasp, 3s. French morocco extra gilt, 2s. 6d.; with rims and clasp, 3s.; with E. and G., 3s.; with rims and clasp, 3s. 6d. Calf, or morocco 4s.; with rims and clasp, 5s. 6d.; with E. and G., 4s. 6d., with rims and clasp, 6s. Calf or morocco extra gilt, 5s.; with rims and clasp, 6s. 6d.; with E. and G., 5s. 6d.; with rims and clasp, 7s. Velvet, with rims and clasp, 7s. 6d., 10s. 6d., and 13s.; with E. and G., 8s., 11s., and 13s. 6d. Russia, antique, with clasp, 8s. 6d., 10s., 12s. 6d.; with E. and G., 9s. 10s. 6d., 13s., with corners and clasps, 20s.; with E. and G., 20s. 6d. Ivory 14s., 16s., 18s., 20s., and 22s. 6d.; with E. and G., 14s. 6d., 16s. 6d., 18s. 6d., 20s. 6d., and 23s. Morocco antique, with 2 patent clasps, 12s.; with E. and G., 12s. 6d.; with corners and clasps, 18s.; with E. and G., 18s. 6d.

The Epistles and Gospels. *Complete*, cloth, 6d.; roan, 1s. 6d.

"This is one of the best editions we have seen of one of the best of all our Prayer Books. It is well printed in clear, large type, on good paper."—*Catholic Opinion.* A very complete arrangement of this which is emphatically the Prayer Book of every Catholic household. It is as cheap as it is good, and we heartily recommend it."—*Universe.* "Two striking features are the admirable order displayed throughout the book, and the insertion of the Indulgences in small type above Indulgenced Prayers. In the Devotions for Mass, the editor has, with great discrimination, drawn largely on the Church's Prayers, as given us in the Missal."—*Weekly Register.*

R. Washbourne, 18 *Paternoster Row, London.*

www.ingramcontent.com/pod-product-compliance
Lightning Source LLC
Chambersburg PA
CBHW030816230426
43667CB00008B/1248